"Thank you, thank you for this book. ... person-
ally warm and wonderful, caring and smart, but this is the side of
the story that we have been missing — the real teacher speaking,
not another westerner reporting well or poorly that his head was
blown off."

> — James Fadiman Ph.D., author and former president of The
> Association for Transpersonal Psychology

"This remarkable and beautiful book suggests a path back to understanding the profound healing and spiritual powers that are here
for us in the plant world. This extraordinary book shows a way
toward reawakening our respect for the natural world, and thus for
ourselves. I pray that we are not too proud, not too entitled, not
too arrogant to heed the invitation."

> — John Robbins, author of *The Food Revolution*, *Diet For A
> New America*, and many other bestsellers

Don José Campos has a free spirit, a generous heart, and deep
knowledge about Amazonian plants, in particular about the
shamanic brew ayahuasca. And he tells good stories in a casual
style. He speaks from experience, and champions simplicity and
humility. I enjoyed his book for all these reasons.

> — Jeremy Narby, Ph.D., author of *The Cosmic Serpent: DNA
> and the Origins of Knowledge*

"*The Shaman & Ayahuasca* brings us a fascinating look at a rich and unfortunately vanishing world of knowledge and spirit, where humans, plants, and the cosmos meet."

— Howard Rheingold, futurist, co-author of *Exploring the World of Lucid Dreaming* with Stephen Laberge, co-author of *Higher Creativity: Liberating the Unconscious for Breakthrough Insights* with Willis Harman

"A uniquely valuable record of the thoughts and recollections of a traditional Amazonian healer, now inexorably enmeshed in the modern world, and the reactions of those who have met and worked with him. This brief book is filled with both knowledge and wisdom, and should be read by anyone with an interest in the unique healing culture of the Upper Amazon."

— Stephan V. Beyer, author of *Singing to the Plants: A Guide to Mestizo Shamanism in the Upper Amazon*

"Weaving together a poignant memoir with practical insights on the shamanic path, Don José Campos offers readers a captivating and deeply personal glimpse into the living practice of Amazonian curanderismo."

— ST Frequency, RealitySandwich.com

JOURNEYS TO SACRED REALMS

The Shaman
& Ayahuasca

DON JOSÉ CAMPOS

With Introduction by CHARLES GROB, M.D.
Translated by ALBERTO ROMAN
Edited and Compiled by GERALDINE OVERTON

DIVINE
ARTS

Published by DIVINE ARTS

DivineArtsMedia.com

An imprint of Michael Wiese Productions

12400 Ventura Blvd. #1111

Studio City, CA 91604

(818) 379-8799, (818) 986-3408 (FAX)

Cover design: Johnny Ink

Cover Painting: Pablo Amaringo

Book Layout: William Morosi

Editor: Geraldine Overton

Photography: Geraldine Overton

Manufactured in the United States of America

Copyright 2011 by Don José Campos

Library of Congress Cataloging-in-Publication Data

Campos, Don José, 1959-

The shaman & ayahuasca : journeys to sacred realms / Don José Campos ; with introduction by Charles Grob, M.D. ; translated by Alberto Roman ; edited and compiled by Geraldine Overton.

p. cm.

Includes bibliographical references.

ISBN 978-1-61125-003-9

1. Shamanism. 2. Ayahuasca ceremony. 3. Hallucinogenic drugs and religious experience. I. Roman, Alberto, 1947- II. Overton, Geraldine, 1957- III. Title. IV. Title: The shaman and ayahuasca.

GN475.8.C36 2011

299.8'142--dc22

2011002843

This book is dedicated to my mother,
my teachers: Don Wilfredo Tuanama, Dona Sarela,
Don Solon, Don Ricardo Peso, Don Guillermo Ojanama
and to the teachings of La Madrecita.

Gracias

Table of Contents

Editor's Notes

THIS BOOK WAS COMPILED from interviews and conversations
recorded over a period of two weeks in September 2009. Michael
Wiese, Alberto Roman and I, were invited by Don José Campos to
join him in Pucallpa, Peru where he lives. From there we journeyed
down the Aquaytia River to a maloca deep in the jungle, and to
Iquitos where we met his teacher, Don Solon and his good friend,
Julio Arce Hidalgo.

The book was originally conceived as containing solely the transmission of Don José, but as the journey unfolded, it became apparent
that the experiences we were having were giving us direct lessons on
how Ayahuasca manifests within our consciousness. It was, therefore,
agreed that some of our experiences ought to be included in the
book to illustrate the words of Don José.

The structure was designed in three parts. In the first part, Don José
takes us gently through the nature of his work, his healings, his
teachers, and his garden. In the second part, Michael, Alberto and

I introduce you to Don José's friends, the visionary painter, Pablo Amaringo, his teacher, Don Solon and his friend the biochemist, Julio Arce Hidalgo. We also include an Ayahuasca ceremony, including the visionary experiences of each of us. This addition will give those of you unfamiliar with the ritual ceremony of Ayahuasca a clearer picture of what it entails. In the third and final section, Don José resumes his transmission and discusses the nature of the expansion of Ayahuasca usage, the various ways Ayahuasca manifests healings and the nature of the illumination of death that we receive while working with her.

You will find that what Don José transmits is *confianza*, deep confidence in the value of his work and gratitude for what "La Madrecita," the spirit of Ayahuasca, offers us.

This project was a life-changing experience for each of us. In addition to this book, the outcome resulted in Michael's documentary, *The Shaman and Ayahuasca*, which has received the "Best Documentary Film" award at the Albuquerque Film Festival.

Michael and I offer these efforts to Don José with love and gratitude for opening up vast new worlds and showing us a far greater understanding of what it means to be a human being living as one with the earth and the cosmos. *Gracias.*

Geraldine Overton-Wiese
Cornwall, UK

Introduction

Charles S. Grob, M.D.

IN RECENT YEARS, increasing interest has been drawn to the remote Amazon rainforest. Sole repository of one-third of the world's plant and animal species, the Amazon has also been home to a great number of natural medicinal compounds, many of which have unfortunately been lost to modern civilization with the relentless erosion of native cultures and traditional knowledge. Yet, one of the great mysteries of the Amazon has survived, and over the past few decades has become manifest to the outside world. This book of reflections, composed by the Peruvian indigenous curandero, Don José Campos, seeks to share with this growing audience his knowledge and wisdom, accrued over many years working with the legendary plant brew, ayahuasca.

Ayahuasca is a decoction of two plants native to the Amazon Forest, Banisteriopsis caapi and Psychotria viridis. When either plant is ingested by itself, it achieves no noticeable effect. However, when the two plants are brewed together for many hours, they induce an extraordinary several hour long visionary state. Prized by the native people as the Great Medicine of the Forest, and used for millennia for purposes of healing, divination and cultural cohesion, its use was forced underground by the arrival of the Spanish and Portuguese invaders during the 16th and 17th Centuries. Determined to eradicate native cultures and force conversion of the native people to Christianity, the newly arrived Europeans identified the plethora of plant hallucinogens they found as tools of the Devil, and condemned their use to the harshest punishments of the Inquisition. While utilization of these plants and the ancient traditions they were integral to remained extant, they could do so only in great secret, and often in disguised form. Indeed, it was not until the mid-20th Century, through the explorations of the great Harvard ethnobotanist, Richard Evans Schultes, that the existence of ayahuasca was revealed to the modern world.

Since the 1980s, the tools of modern laboratory science have been applied to unravel some of the mysteries of ayahuasca. Western scientists, including ethnobotanist and pharmacologist Dennis McKenna, have determined that ayahuasca's psychoactivity is attributable to the biochemical interaction between the biologically active alkaloids in Banisteriopsis and Psychotria. While the powerful hallucinogenic alkaloid dimethyltryptamine (DMT) present in Psychotria is rapidly inactivated in the gut by the monoamine oxidase (MAO) enzyme system, when slowly brewed over many hours with Banisteriopsis, the monoamine oxidase inhibiting (MAOI) action of the harmala alkaloids in the Banisteriopsis deactivates enzymatic degradation and allows for absorption and central nervous system activation of the

DMT. How the native peoples of the Amazon discovered this highly unusual interaction between these two plants is another mystery. Whether through some form of divine inspiration, as many have conjectured, or through the rigorous trial and error experimentation with the vast regional plant life over centuries before coming upon this remarkable and highly unique interaction, its origins will never be known. Yet the extraordinary effects ayahuasca is capable of inducing bring to mind the legendary cities of gold the conquistadors sought for in vain, never realizing that these tales of dazzling jewels and precious metals apparently were metaphors for the astonishing alterations of inner landscapes of consciousness brought about by these sacred, visionary plants.

While the knowledge and indeed the use of ayahuasca has spread in recent years to North America and Europe, as well as earlier in the 20th Century to urban Brazil where it has been utilized as a psychoactive sacrament in ceremony of modern syncretic religions, its core use has remained in the region of its origins, the lush, biologically diverse and remote Amazon Basin. To optimally understand the ancient traditions and belief systems from which ayahuasca emerged, it is necessary to examine its indigenous context. Don José Campos, Peruvian vegetalista-curandero, grandson of a traditional ayahuasca healer and son of a modern western-trained physician, presents in his book "The Shaman and Ayahuasca" a compelling perspective on the core principles and world view acquired over his many years of study and practical application.

While modern man and woman have often discounted and trivialized the knowledge of native peoples, such hubris is shattered upon encountering the legendary visionary plants of the rain forest. Ayahuasca, while of inestimable value for many who have experienced its effects, is not for the faint of heart. It calls for courage, inner strength and discipline. Don José emphasizes the need for La Dieta, strict sexual abstinence and prohibition of processed foods, salt, sugar, beef and pork, as well as alcohol and many drugs. While concomitant use of marijuana often occurs in North America and Europe, as well as the Santo Daime Church of Brazil, Don José many years ago in conversation told me that "the spirit of the ayahuasca and the spirit of the marijuana do not get along". And given the frequency of prescription drug use in modern times, particular caution may need to be taken with certain medications. One highly popular class of pharmaceuticals that represents a significant risk for adverse drug-ayahuasca interaction, is the SSRI (selective serotonin re-uptake inhibitor) antidepressants. Pharmacologist J.C. Callaway and I have published in the medical literature our concerns that such a combination may induce a serotonin syndrome, a potentially serious medical condition. Disregarding the important dietary and behavioral prohibitions understood by native peoples over centuries of use as essential for ensuring safety and optimizing outcome, or mindlessly combining modern pharmaceuticals with these powerful ancient plants, significantly enhances the level of risk users may expose themselves to.

The implications of these ancient technologies to alter consciousness and the knowledge learned from such inner explorations pose a challenge to modern science and culture. These "other-worldly" experiences, acquired from people we have customarily relegated to the role of "primitive", also offer us hope in a world suffused with danger. These are teaching plants, and the lineage of those versed in understanding their myriad effects are from the tribal peoples of the forest. That their secret knowledge and technologies are emerging into the modern world during this time of global peril is a blessing of inestimable proportion to humanity. With widespread environmental devastation, staggering economic disparities, unceasing violent conflict throughout the world and frightening arsenals of conventional and nuclear weaponry, the human race, along with all the species of the earth, stand on the brink of annihilation. During this time of peril, we have suddenly and unexpectedly found ourselves recipients of these ancient plant technologies, gifts from the earth designed to instruct humanity how it may save the planet. Indeed, as I once heard a wise man say, it is remarkable that by ingesting plants we learn to become more human.

In the ancient Quechua Indian language, the word ayahuasca is translated as "Vine of the Soul," or "Vine of the Dead". The ayahuasca experience offers us the opportunity to confront our own existential reality, and push us to the realization and appreciation that all life is both finite and eternal. By confronting our own symbolic death we experience profound healing, of self, relationship and community. Wise teachers, such as Don José, have emerged to instruct us in how to respond to the ever-looming crisis to humanity. They are the linkage to the wisdom of our ancestors, who beseech us to wake up, open our eyes and begin the healing essential for there to be a future world inhabited by our descendents. "The Shaman and Ayahuasca" provides us with essential information as we embark on this path.

Charles S. Grob, MD is a professor of psychiatry and biobehavioral sciences at UCLA's David Geffen School of Medicine, and is Director of the Division of Child and Adolescent Psychiatry at Harbor-UCLA Medical Center. He is also a founding board member and Director of Clinical Research for The Heffter Institute, a non-profit organization dedicated to the scientific study of psychedelics. Grob has held a long-standing interest in altered mind states and the healing power that they may have. He conducted the first FDA-approved study giving MDMA to human subjects, and recently completed a research investigation of the safety and efficacy of psilocybin in the treatment of anxiety in patients with advanced-stage cancer. He has also led an international team of experts looking into the long-term effects of ayahuasca use by Brazilian members of the União do Vegetal church, finding beneficial effects on those with substance addiction problems.

A Greeting from
Don José

Beautiful People!

We are going to take a journey together and by the end of the
journey you will recognize the subtle changes that the spirit of
Ayahuasca, La Madrecita, is offering you.

Books are fine, books are OK, but the understanding of Ayahuasca
will not be in the words. The spirit of Ayahuasca will come to you
through my intention, my energy, for this is what a shaman does, he
transmits energy and healing through his songs, through his presence
and with the help of spirits who he calls upon through his *icaros*.

This little book will not be full of facts, for Ayahuasca is a mystery
and cannot be held down to facts. There are many books that try to
explain Ayahuasca (many very interesting and very good) because we
in the Western world like facts. Our brains like certainty and explana-
tions, but let me tell you right here, Ayahuasca cannot come to you

in this way. She does not enter your brain from the left side. She is global. She lights up your entire brain. You make communication harder when you approach her with your left brain, so relax, breathe and let me sing you a few songs. Let me tell you a few stories of how I began working with her. With a few little jokes here and there, we will laugh together and we will meet some of my friends, and by the end of our time together, without you knowing it, you will have had my transmission to you.

My friends, let me say that after many years working with Ayahuasca I can see that interest in her has grown incredibly. People are coming to her from Europe, Japan, China, Israel and Palestine.... The expansion is very, very large and ongoing. But why? I have asked myself this many times. Why now? Why are you so important now?

This is the question we must think about very carefully.

CHAPTER 1

Are You a Shaman?

So LET ME BEGIN by saying that in the tradition here in the Amazon the word shaman does not exist. What does exist is another name, *vegetalista* because the vegetalistas work with plants. There is also another way of saying it, which is *curandero*. If you ask the old curanderos around here, "Are you a shaman?" They will say, "No, I am a vegetalista." I prefer to be called a vegetalista because I also work with the plants. Ayahuasca is one among many.

The world of shamanism is something else altogether. I will begin to explain by telling you about a vision I had with one of my teachers.

Here in the jungle, the curanderos or vegetalistas who drink the plants do so partly to acquire their power. This power or force is called *mariri*. It means the power of the plants you have taken.

In an Ayahuasca ceremony with one of my teachers, I could see the power of the plants inside his body. So with his song, his icaro, he began to call forth the power, not only of the plants, but of animals as well. He invoked the power of the *otorongo*, the jaguar. In the vision I was having of him, I could see him place the spirit of the jaguar in the person he was healing, to protect him. This spirit or energy was transmitted through his icaro.

It is here that we step into the world of shamanic forces because the shaman has the power to invoke these energies, these spirits. One can clearly see the power of protection. It was not just me. The person involved also saw the protection. He came out of the ceremony healed and stronger and with a lot more energy. To me, that is shamanic.

It is through drinking the plants that one can obtain this force and the transfer of this force is shamanic.

Of course, I have the vision because I drink the plants. So from being a curandero, a vegetalista, one is able to acquire all the forces of the plants. Then you have the possibility of invoking the powers of the animals, and with your intention, you pass it on to people for their healing.

It's very important to understand that how you say things has power. One's intention and how one says it, what's behind the intention and the faith one has in the intention, all these things contribute to the healing. And if you have faith and you want to heal somebody and if your intention is clear and pure and clean, then even just a cup of water can heal! Of course it's even better if you drink the plants because then, with gratitude and the right intention you have even more power!

One becomes a vegetalista by experimenting or by transmission from ancestors. Our Mother Earth offers us this garden of plants. Our ancestors transmit their experience to us and, of course, we experiment.

In my case, from my father's side and because my grandfather was a vegetalista-curandero, it is in my blood. This knowledge of the plants, though I was never seeking it, I knew it was in me. So when I began drinking the plants it was very easy. It was easy for me to understand, to be very sensitive.

My observation with other healers, including a couple of my teachers, is that they entered the world of vegetalistas seeking their own healing.

One of my teachers, for instance, was an alcoholic for 40 years. He was homeless. One day someone suggested that he try some plants. My teacher replied, "Plants? I am already working with sugar cane!" He did not believe.

This man admitted himself into the jungle. The vegetalista said to him, "Do you want to be healed or not?" My teacher said, "If you heal me great, if not…?"

"Come to a purge then," said the vegetalista. By the way, in the language of vegetalistas we do not use the word "ceremony" we use the word purge.

Well, the man purged. The vegetalista said to him, "What you are throwing up is all the illness that is in your body. You vomited your sickness as an alcoholic."

My teacher was astounded. He had a rebirth. He did not want to return to the city. "Now I want to be healed!" He remained in the jungle doing diets, meditating. As he remained in this place he began to feel the voices of the spirits of the plants. Icaros came to him. His life changed. From that point he left alcohol behind and became a curandero. This is what my teacher told me about how he became a healer. There are no coincidences here.

He is now dead, but he was a great teacher.

I will introduce you to another great teacher of mine who lives in Iquitos. His name is Don Solon. As a young man he developed an eye problem, a cataract perhaps. He had a hard a time. He did not believe in any of this either.

The hospital could not do anything for him so his wife suggested that he go see a *curioso*, another term for curandero. This curioso invited him to drink Ayahuasca. There was some healing but more than this he discovered he had the potential to be a curandero. So he began to investigate. He began to drink the plants.

I respect him tremendously. He became a great shaman. Once you meet him you will see. He is a very humble man yet he transmits great confidence and tranquillity.

So, some of us have it in our blood, but I never looked for it. Maybe they were not looking for it either, but their illness took them to drink the plants to become vegetalistas. While this is a common way to get into the work, fewer still have it in the blood.

In my case, when I began drinking the plants I discovered the potential that I had, but even more, I began my own healing. Who does not have problems? I went though a lot of pain, sadness, sorrow, hatreds, a lot of afflictions. I released them slowly. In this manner the plants were my teachers and continue to be.

It is important to understand that one is not ingesting a liquid, one is ingesting the spirit of the plant. One then acquires the mariri and one advances spiritually. With the plants the process of spiritual advancement is accelerated. One enters the world of the spirit of plants, the world of the spirits of the animals. One enters the world of the spirit of the elements: Fire, Air, Earth and Water. Plants will accelerate one's understanding of these things. Yes, the plants will take us to this level.

The sweet thing about curanderismo is that in this knowledge there are no sects. It has nothing to do with religion. It is free. Fluid. There is a difference between religion and religiosity. The religious part is the practice. Remember, when we do an Ayahuasca practice it is religious but it has nothing to do with religion.

When I partake and share Ayahuasca I am sharing the wisest of the wise. At times during ceremony, people can confront what we could call their own "demons" or negative energies. This has to take place in a religious context. As you know, we take Ayahuasca in a group setting. There we release our masks and expose our real selves. When you go to church you might do it hypocritically. Not here. Here you will vomit, cleanse, and quite often support each other in that. That is how it should be. Accept one another. That is what I like about it. I am not a practitioner of any religion, but I am very religious about my knowledge of plants. That is my practice. That is what gives me strength spiritually and mentally. And it extends my life. My consciousness is expanded so I can understand at various levels.

That is why I like taking the plants. I become very sensitive. All my senses are open, amplified, and it is even better when we do the ceremony in nature. We can smell, feel, breathe, see and hear better. The most subtle and refined sensibilities are there. From the delicate sounds of the forest — that is where the orchestra begins. From there you will find all the musical instruments. When I take Ayahuasca I say, "Oh, they are playing the *charanguito*, they are playing the flute, they are giving me a few words, they bring me these gifts and say, "Here, compose!"

So, thank you to the plants, thank you, Ayahuasca, thank you, Mother Earth. That is the gratitude.

Of course, there are other ways, other practices that can be used to gain access to the knowledge and wisdom one gains from Ayahuasca but with the plants, it's an accelerated curriculum, an accelerated course, if you will. Yes, there are other ways, for example, meditation. But it might take you years to attain what one can gain in one ceremony. That's why I like the plants. They are very fast.

Sometimes I see myself like a tree and I feel that throughout my body there are other little trees growing, and also little animals are walking by, and little birds are singing, teaching me the icaros, and when I look at my veins they are like little vines. And I feel that vibration in other people. That's what Ayahuasca transmits. It's like a blessing. It is a blessing. And there is a continuous growth.

The other day I met this gentleman who was doing a lot of *dietas*, a lot of diets. So I began to look at his body, to see inside his body and he said, "You know I'm getting tired and weary of taking plants." But I said to him, "Wait! With each plant that you're taking, you are making them grow in your body. And once you have understood that, then your heart will open and the knowledge will come forth." So when he took the Ayahuasca, he began to see his own mariri and the mariri of the plants. Do you remember when I told you about the mariri? The mariri is the power. Can you get that? Yes, okay, cool. He saw his own power and the power of the plants. Very nice, no? He began to sing icaros from the mariris. The songs came to him. So I only gave him two words. "Allow growth." It's growing, it's growing. That's all. Two words. And with that, he left with strength and power.

Yeah.

How delicious, how nice!

CHAPTER 2

Like a Jaguar

THE FIRST TIME I DRANK AYAHUASCA, it was for me something incomprehensible, very incomprehensible. I felt insane, crazy. I saw myself like an animal, like a jaguar, like a serpent, an eagle, and sometimes like a condor. And I was saying to myself, "I'm crazy, crazy!" I observed my body. It was like a very primitive animal. It was something that I couldn't share. I said, "God! I'm crazy, I'm crazy!" In those days I couldn't understand it. I couldn't comprehend it. But as I went along drinking Ayahuasca and other plants, I began to understand.

That first time was very hard for me, very, very difficult. Because in that moment you don't know what's going on. I remember that a curandero sang and called the elements and called the animals. I could see them. "Is it real? What is it? What is it?"

Yeah, I thought I was going crazy ... but slowly, I began to comprehend it. In reality, it's not that I'm crazy ... well, maybe a little bit ... but during those states, I went through moments of ... I'm not going to call it hell, because hell is the kind of word that has been utilized too much by the religious people. So I won't use that word. Let's call it "a dark world". It was horrible. There was a moment when I fainted, I lost consciousness altogether. I thought I might die, but if I die, I die ... what am I to do? That was just something I was thinking because, if you're dying, you're not going to remember that you're dying. But something else was dying ... something of mine was dying. That's why I went to those underworlds, those dark worlds. And then I began to vomit. And in the vomit I could see monsters and that was scary. But I had nothing to do but be grateful, thank the monsters. "Thank you, because you've taken me up to this point so I can be free of you. So thank you." That was one of the crises, strong crises that I have lived.

The initiation continues, it doesn't just stay there. This is my way of seeing it. Sometimes in this life it is as if we are like an onion. You peel one layer, you peel another layer, you peel another layer, you peel another layer, and when does it stop? Yes? So we're always in a state of learning, learning, learning, it's endless. And that's what's good about Ayahuasca. She knows when to bring out the illness or the negativity that you have, she knows when to take it out of you, she knows the moment. That's why I'm telling you it's a mysterious plant.

At the same time she knows when to place you in divine realms. Yes, absolutely she knows. When the moment is ready she will give that to you. She will place you in the realms that are appropriate for you, at a level that is appropriate for you.

Recently, I had the good fortune of having a dear friend visit me. She taught me a lot about the work and her name is Alice Walker.[*] She visited me to do a dieta. She is very lovely.

One of the things we talked about is subtlety. "The plants teach through subtlety," she said. So I'm going to tell you a story.

A curandero had a very difficult problem. He had already taken some healing plants and he thought that if that dose could work, a larger dose would work even better. He would be totally healed! But when he almost died, he realized this was not so. What does that teach us? The plants teach you about subtlety. He said, "I realised I made a mistake. All it takes is a little root. That's enough. Why did I put in twenty-two roots? It's not necessary!" And I tell you this because Alice taught me to look at the subtlety of plants.

The aroma of flowers is very subtle. That itself is a teaching. We have to be open enough so that the teaching can come into us. Alice, she would stand up and she would take some leaves and she'd begin to sing. Ah, look what she's teaching us!

This leads me into a discussion of dosage.

---

[*] American author and poet best known for the critically acclaimed novel, "The Color Purple" for which she won the Pulitzer Prize for Fiction and which was adapted into a critically acclaimed film of the same name, as well as a Broadway musical. Her work typically concerns the struggles of women against a sexist and racist society and the role of women of color in history. Alice Walker is a respected figure in the liberal political community for her support of her sometimes, unpopular views. Her activism, begun during the time of the Civil Rights Movement when she attended the 1963 March on Washington, has continued to the present time, protesting the war in Iraq and working to persuade Israel and Egypt to open their borders into Gaza.

Many people have asked me, "How do you determine the proper dosage for each person during an Ayahuasca ceremony?"

Well, to tell the truth I just feel it, it's pure intuition. I gauge the dose just by the feel of the person. I can look at them and think, "He needs just a little bit," or "She will need a larger dose." Sometimes people come to the ceremony with the idea that the more they drink the more things are going to happen! This is not how Ayahuasca works. Sometimes the most important visions and the most important healings come with just a little bit.

Sometimes, you know, your physical body does not want to take it. It totally rebels, rejects it. But the spirit does want it. The soul does want it because the soul wants the healing. It wants the cleansing, the purification. It is because of our rationality, our reason, that we have such a reaction, but the soul does want it because it needs it. It needs it so it can calm down, so it can be tranquil. The spirit of your soul wants to expunge or throw out something in the physical body that is not good for you. That's what I see. That's why I like it.

While Ayahuasca is a purge, not everyone experiences that kind of cleansing. People often go where they need to go according to their inner work. Some folks experience other realms that are celestial and benevolent. At other times, the same person may experience what they consider a dark realm, which is frightening to them, but afterward they will realize that La Madrecita gave them a powerful healing with deep understanding and insights. She always gives you what you need at the time.

CHAPTER 3

A Soplada

Now, I am going to take you through a *soplada*, a healing. This is done through the song or through the icaro, which we will talk about a little bit later on.

(José expels air through his mouth, takes a mouthful of *agua florida* and sprays the scented water into the air and begins to sing.)

(* translation)

Ayahuasca, Ayahuasquita   *Ayahuasca Mother of all Plants*

Mamancura yari-ri   *The power of your medicine*

Sinchi sinchi medicina yari-ri   *Cleanses my body / Cleanses my*

Limpia limpia cuerpcito yari-ri   *spirit*

Limpia limpia espirito yari-ri

Sinchi sinchi medicina yari-ri   *The power of your medicine*

Sinchi sinchi Icarito yari-ri   *The power of the Icaro*

Chuya chuya medicina yari-ri   *Pure white medicine*

Tukui Tukui almacita yari-ri   *Cleanses your soul*

Tukui Tukui huanquincito   *Cleanses you my brother and my*

yar-ri....*   *sister....*

(José continues to sing this icaro for about 10 minutes, asking the plant spirits, the earth, to heal. He asks for blessings from the earth and expresses gratitude for the plants and medicines. He finishes the song and begins to spray and blow agua florida.)

I am going to explain a little bit about this process.

Now, in the first part I'm cleansing, I'm purifying. I cleanse myself in order to prepare to enter into that space. Then I cleanse the person I am healing.

The first thing I cleanse is the person's corona, his crown chakra, then his back, because the back is where the energy surges up so you have to protect it.

Then the heart follows, then the solar plexus, that whole region, afterwards the hands. These are different energy potentials I am addressing.

What's the special power of the solar plexus? Why am I going there?

Because that is where the energies actually enter.

The hands we cleanse because we're always touching everything and in this kind of work, the hands have to be cleansed. And after the cleansing the icaros follow and that's when the real healing begins.

With the icaros, I'm invoking the mother of the plants. I invoke Ayahuasca's mother. Not the plants, but the mothers of the plants. In Quechua, Ayahuasca is called *ay mama*. I am asking the mother of the plants to come and heal the illness, whatever illness the person has in his body. That's what I am invoking. At the same time I am protecting him. Sometimes the healing is done with tobacco or flow-ered water, sometimes with camphor. All of this helps in the healing. This is an overall healing. It is not specific to any particular illness. All of this is done in the moment. There is really no rational way to think about it. The important thing to understand is that there is a transfer of my energy to the person I'm healing. The energy is the intention that's been transferred with the spirit.

When I sing an icaro I am calling the spirits of the plants or the animal, and they come, and I transfer the energy to the patient through the song, through the icaro. And that energy, that spirit that is left behind in the person I am healing, will continue to heal him even after the ceremony is over.

In some cases where conventional medicine cannot understand what is going on, the curandero's use of the icaros can be very powerful when sung with intention. For example, recently my son was ill with vomiting and diarrhoea. He was very restless so he was taken to the doctor. The doctor prescribed medicine for the vomiting and diarrhoea but it didn't work. I said, "Bring him to me. I'm going to do a tobacco healing and sing to him." He was crying and he was nervous and it calmed him down. It also calmed down the vomiting and I gave him a plant called *canela*, cinnamon. It was like I wiped away his illness without using any kind of prescription medicine. It was quick. I have seen it in my son and I have seen it in other people and in other settings. What's great about these plants, these ways of healing, is that they are so ancient. This is our traditional medicine.

I'll tell you about my experience in the early days. I was born out in the country. In order to get to the city it would take two days

and two nights. There were no doctors. What would my mother do
when I got sick? She would use plants. She would gather the plants
and sing. She would cook the plants and often she would sing to us
as we drank the plants as well. During that time there was no way
to get access to doctors so, out of necessity, one had to maintain
contact with the plants and know how to use them. This kind of
healing goes back hundreds and hundreds of years. The way I see
it … sometimes they would go and gather the plants without really
knowing what they were doing. They would just get the plants and
the only thing that would matter were the effects, the results. In
some cases, a curandero would come and do a healing, but at other
times, out of sheer necessity, one would have to know how to use
the plants.

Another story I can tell you.

There was a gentleman who had been stung by a stingray. You can
imagine, it would take a day or more to travel from the country to
the city. So obviously the question was, "What was to be done?"
I watched them and I learned a lot. They gathered very fragrant,
strong smelling plants and they cooked them, boiled them. And just
with the vapour of the plant, the poison was extracted. Just with the
vapours. And the thing is, there were results. They didn't have to take
him to a hospital. Again, it's out of necessity that forces this kind of
practice in plant medicines.

This knowledge comes from our grandfathers and our grandmothers
and I can verify that these things work. I can tell you any number
of stories. I have even seen snakebites cured by using plants. When
a woman I knew had been bitten by a snake, they went to look for

the curandero. And then the curandero began to look for the plants. When he had found the plants he began to sing. He boiled the plants and then he placed them very near the wound. And slowly the venom ... it was very interesting for me to observe this ... slowly the venom was extracted.

I also found another very curious thing that these folk practitioners say. They say that when this kind of animal bites you, primarily serpents, what they often suggest, is to maintain the patient in an isolated area. Very isolated. So that certain kinds of people will not approach the patients who have had sexual intercourse. If those folks have had sexual relations, the person who has been bitten by the snake will become altered. They will go crazy. Fever will come. And that's just curious, all of that. They say that there are effects that the snake bitten person can feel even up to a hundred meters away. I have seen the effects and I can verify it. I asked that curandero, "Why is this woman getting worse?" And he said to me, "There are some people here, who have come by, who have had sexual relations."

I will say something else regarding the cure of my son. Children are so sensitive. There's a word we use here, a common term used by the elders, even the curanderos, the word is *manchari*. Manchari is always something that makes an impression upon you or frightens you. That's the way we say it, "Oh! This child has the manchari." Also, sometimes, we say that person, or that lady has given the other person the manchari. *Susto* is the Spanish word for it. In English you would say, "To take a fright."

My son had taken a fright and he had gotten it from somebody.

Another practice to note is that during ceremony, I will use lemon and salt. What I'm doing there with the lemon and the salt is that I'm diminishing the effects of the Ayahuasca, the effects of the experience you are having. I'm going to talk a little bit about cinnamon too. Here, the way we explain it is by asking the way the plants function, and what is their spirit. You know when you have tasted cinnamon, you've experienced a sensation of heat or numbing. So this plant they relate to the spirit of fire. And also when you take it, you feel the heat in your body... in your stomach. In the case with the manchari or the susto, your body is cold because when you have a fright the fright causes the body to become cold. So with the song and the medicine, in this case cinnamon, you seek to reheat the body. You can also observe when someone's ears become really pale, or almost transparent, people will say, "Oh, that person is scared, that person has the fright." All of this is based on observation. It's the empirical method we were talking about earlier. But what's important is that it's effective. You are provided with the plants, one sings, and you're out of your problem. When I gave my son the plant to drink he was crying ... then he went to sleep. It relaxed him. And he was happy. Why give him antibiotics? It wasn't necessary. Generally, conventional medicine doesn't understand this process, but it's effective. It's a kind of science. It's more a science of the lived.

CHAPTER 4

Icaros

So, HOW DID I COME BY MY OWN ICAROS? When I started participating in dietas my teachers would just give me assorted plants and
leave me alone.

I would say to him, "Why, Maestro, why my teacher are you aban-
doning me?" Because the practice was that he just gave me the plants
to drink and then would leave me by myself. The only thing that my
teacher would say was, "Take the plants, drink the plants. The plants
are going to speak to you." But in my rational mind I was thinking,
"How are the plants going to talk to me?" Days went by and I began
to have dreams, and from there I understood that plants really were
speaking to me. That's when the icaros began to come to me. You
know, I didn't know how to speak Quechua before this. But the
plants taught me. Pablo said the same thing. I think the melody actually comes from the animals. All you do is just incorporate in your
body whatever you're receiving. Then the words show up.

My icaros do change over time. I want to explain what icaro means. Icaro, in the language of the vegetalistas means, "healing". With the icaro I'm going to heal you. With the icaro I'm going to make you sane. As you take the plants, you acquire the mariri, which is an inner power that when matured, and combined with a song, is what makes the icaro effective.

When I sing my icaros they are not for specific illnesses. I think people who are selling you icaros for specific illnesses, at least in my take on things, are ripping you off. The icaros do not work that way. I know that it is in fashion at the moment, but you know, opportunists are taking people in.

So what is the Shamanic practice then? First, with the song or with the icaro, invoke the power, be that of an animal or the power of a plant, and they do come to help you. As you have seen in the work of Pablo Amaringo, the "little doctors" in his paintings are the spirits of the plants. They arrive to perform their operations. You call them through the icaros. The icaros are conduits for the power.

The "whoosh" you hear after the end of an icaro means that you have released a particular energy from the group. Even in the beginning of the ceremony when I whisper into the bottle, that's an icaro. I'm going to add something more to the icaro question to show how they work.

Sometimes I see that an icaro can be annoying to some folks. Or sometimes the icaro is provoking or evoking all your problems and sometimes people have told me, "Stop! Stop! Please stop singing!" But I don't listen to them. Because I know what's happening. The icaro is energy and intention. And the intention is to heal. And sometimes, with some people, certain folks, the icaro is actually making you vomit. And another time, it can take you way up. Yes. The same icaro can do all of this. Yes, the same one. Yeah. Yeah. Up, down, it'll take you to all kinds of places. Yes, that's Shamanism, the moving of those energies.

By the way, hearing a recording of an icaro does not have the same effect. For instance, it's always more enjoyable when Alberto joins me in the ceremony because when I'm singing and playing with him the energy is occurring in the moment. The recording, well, it's already done. In the ceremony the music is occurring in the moment, for the moment and as the moment.

Pablo said a reproduction of his painting contains only ¼ of the power of the original. It's the same principal. Yeah, it's the same. It's the same energy so it's analogous. You guys are getting this! Great!

I am very respectful of icaros. I never sing an icaro outside the context. In some things as you can see, I'm very, very disciplined. It's like tobacco … I only use tobacco in the ceremonies because I know tobacco is sacred. It's the same thing with songs because they're healing songs. It's like Pablo's painting when he says to keep the painting veiled to bring the energy up.

The icaros do require something of me for them to be powerful yet in my experience, you know, what I do is to allow the icaro to flow. So, very often when I sing the icaro, it's by inspiration. It doesn't work if it's like a mathematical or structured thing. It's just what comes to me in the moment. I feel this is the appropriate response, the right invocation. Singing icaros just makes me happy, happy in the knowledge that I am able to assist someone, to help someone heal and to open up worlds for them.

I am so grateful to Ayahuasca. I wasn't a musician. I didn't know anything. I didn't know how to play one single instrument. But thanks to Ayahuasca, she gave me the inspiration and opened me up. I'm not a painter, but perhaps with music, or with the words or the songs, that's how I paint. So Ayahuasca is my inspiration. And because of that I've been able to transmit to other people who have often been frightened to express themselves. And that was the best way to say, "Okay, now you express yourself! Open up! Don't be afraid!" So, thanks to Ayahuasca I am more sensitive and creative.

Do I have a favourite icaro? No. I don't have a favourite one. Music is made in the moment. Sometimes when I begin the Ayahuasca cere-monies, I sing songs from my *Maestros*, my teachers. At other times I sing my own. But often when I'm in trance, I just explore. I'm feeling what shows up. That's all.

It's very interesting that the icaros tell us where a healing should begin and where the protection should take place. First, it wants to protect the head, then your back then your chest and your hands. The icaro teaches the curandero how to do it and where to start and the information is being transmitted through the song. That's the way the spirits communicate the information, through the songs. The songs come down to us from an old tradition.

Each curandero has the option of adding more information to the body of the song to transmit more knowledge. Also, icaros are timeless. It could be the most ancient song and also the most present. On the front cover of my CD, it says it's the Song of Time.

Remember that in a ceremony, people are putting their trust in someone to guide the ship. I do let people sing at times, but the healing is for them. I play with that a little bit, but not in a frivolous way. It's like a high play.

CHAPTER 5

His Father Returns

ONE OF MY FAVORITE BOOKS, because the man I am about to tell you about has lived it and I'm totally in agreement with him, explains and describes very poetically and very simply this world of shamanism and Ayahuasca. His name is Pablo Calvo and the book is called, "The Three Halves of Ino Moxo." He is from Peru, but now deceased. There is a translation in English. It's a good translation, but the spirit of the work is really in the Spanish version. He says, for instance, something that is enchanting: Many people say that when we go to the jungle there's complete silence. But he says no. The jungle is a perfect harmonic orchestra. So when the jungle begins to sing, when the cicadas begin to sing, those are the vibrations of the chacruna. That's the spirit of chacruna.

That is so true. So when we drink, that is what we feel. There is the "Vrrrroooooooooom!" It is what we experience. And Pablo Calvo says it in a very poetic form, in a very simple way to understand.

Ayahuasca, on the other hand, has a sound that brings the intoxication. There is a word that we use here that does not exist in the

English language. The word is *mareo*. It's like being in the sea, that kind of swerve or seasickness. Sometimes before the ceremony I tell the participants to engage the energy to prepare them for the journey. I say, "Just imagine that we are in the middle of the ocean. Sometimes in the ocean there are storms. Sometimes there are tempests. And we're in a little boat and there inside the mareo some will scream. Some people will be asking for life jackets. The only thing that I ask you to do, is breathe. Let it flow. Become one with the sea. Look at the waves, they come on strong and then they calm down a bit and that's the way to go. Sometimes you have a surfboard, and sometimes you just play with the wave." And in these moments I'm just preparing them for the ride. I tell them to prepare them for what could happen if there's a really powerful ceremony. This adds flavor to the ceremony.

Each curandero, each shaman, prepares the ceremony in whatever way he wants. There are no fixed patterns because one's inspiration sets the ceremony. That is what I like about it. It's free. It's *libre*. Some things are traditional, true, but others are not, they are my own creation. I continue creating.

Tobacco is always part of it, the perfumed water, camphor and the *soplos*. I conduct the ceremonies according to the necessities of the group. Sometimes curanderos are called maestros, which means master or teacher because he knows about the plants and the work. It's out of respect that you say that, but at the same time that he's a master or a teacher, he's always a student. The teacher is always learning because you can never say that he finally got it all. The maestro is always involved in a process of learning.

To me, it's completely experiential and existential. It would be nice if we could take a pill and we could say, with this pill you will immediately attain the highest levels of spirituality, but all you can do is experience it, live it and work it, and the work is to be done each day, day by day. That's why one is always moving between being a teacher and a student, learning from everything.

A good question is: are pharmaceuticals effective since they might not contain the spirit of the plant? Well, then, I'm going to tell you a case study.

A medical doctor friend of mine drank Ayahuasca for many years and other plants as well. He believed he had learnt to be a curandero. So what happened was, a patient came to him with a series of lesions on his body. The doctor asked me, "What do you think he has? Do you think we'll be able to heal him?" I said, "To tell you the truth, I don't know. So let us drink some Ayahuasca, and maybe we will see what we can do." The doctor was convinced that someone had put a curse on this patient. We were trying to heal him, but the poor gentleman was getting worse. I don't know how it came to me but I said, "Why don't we send him to one of our teachers who taught us about the plants. This is not our case." So I took him to a little town and the Maestro immediately saw him. "This is not a problem that a curandero is going to be able to heal. What's going to be helpful here is the pharmacy." So, to the missus of the Maestro, he said, "Go to the pharmacy and get these pills in a little box." And the Maestro began to bless him, to sing. Do you know what the gentleman had? Psoriasis. The pills were cortisone.

The doctor could not see it, but the curandero could! You get it? Do you see? That's funny. But all the master did was bless and sing. So the important thing is intention. No, pharmaceuticals are not bad. Each thing has its functions in the moment. So to me, it is funny that the curandero brought reality back to his friend the doctor, who thought he was a curandero.

So the pharmaceuticals do have a kind of spirit and they have their function. But the thing with the pharmaceuticals is, you also have to know how to ask for the relief, to bring that other experience in. You also have to invoke spirits when you work with the pharmaceuticals and that adds something else to it.

My grandfather was a curandero. My father is a conventional doctor.

Okay, I'm going tell you a bit about my life. My father engendered me, and afterward he left. I don't even carry his name. But that doesn't matter. Ayahuasca healed me from all of that, the resentment and that other stuff … okay. Okay. Good. I'm simply grateful that I'm alive. But he now respects me a lot. What happens with these matters of curanderismo is that I have the opportunity to look at myself. I study myself. Since I was a child I knew my calling, but I've always resisted it. So one day this woman discovered me. She said to me, "You're good for these things."

"For what things?" I said to her.
"You can work with the plants."
"Nah, nah… you're crazy!" I said to her. I didn't take her seriously.
"But I see it in you," she continued. She said, "Don't stop with this work. One day I'm going to invite you to a plant." So she invited me.

I first started with San Pedro. I drank it. To me it was weird. It was strange. I began to see people as skeletons, without flesh. "What's this? This is weird." That's when I opened up. And I drank it fifty times. In those days I did not know Ayahuasca and a friend told me, "There's a plant that's even stronger than San Pedro. Do you want to try it?" "Okay! Why not!" So I took it. I drank a cup and it didn't have any effect. It was like drinking water. The teacher said, "I see nothing's happened to you, but return in three days and then you'll drink again". And so I was opened up. I began to see images like in some of Pablito's paintings. I was seeing teachers and beings talking to me. I thought I was going crazy. At the same time I could also feel so much pain for not having a father who could guide me and accompany me. As I felt that pain and sorrow that's when I began to get it out, and after doing Ayahuasca a lot of times, slowly I began to experience forgiveness. I began to forgive my father for not taking care of me when I needed him. I was grateful for this work. I was also thankful to my father because if I had been taken care of by him, maybe I would have studied to be a doctor. Who knows? Who knows who I would have become? What I feel is that everyone has his own path, his own road. Or what we say here, everyone has his own star.

When I began working with Ayahuasca, I began to know different kinds of people because it changed me. It totally changed me. In those days I was very young. Twenty-seven years is very young! It freed me from being shy. It freed me from hatreds and feelings of sadness. Ayahuasca taught me how to choose my friends. I separated myself from a world I saw as frivolous. I went to pursue this work with plants because I saw my own healing take place. I matured.

One day my father called me. He didn't even know me. He said, "Many people have said that you're like me, I would like to get to know you. One of these days, yes, come visit me and then we will talk."

I visited him. I talked to him. I told him, "Look, I've forgiven you for everything. I don't want to hurt you. I don't have a grudge against you. I know we are related by blood, but we don't have a father-son relationship, and that's true, but what is real is that you and I, we can be good friends." I told him, "This is what I do. I work with plants. Do you want to drink with me?" "Okay," he said. "Que bien, hombre!" "Wow! Cool!" And so he drank. And then he purged. And then he said, "Please forgive me that I didn't help you in anything at all." He said, "Forgive me. I can see that you're very intelligent, and you know this type of healing very well. You know things that psychiatrists don't even understand."

And since then he and I have taken the plants together several times. Well, he respects me a lot and I likewise. I tell him, "You're a doctor of human bodies, but with these plants I heal the souls. That's the difference between our knowledge. You operate on bodies and I work on souls. This is my work. And this is what I'm doing while I'm with you. Ayahuasca is healing us now as we speak. It's working. All those situations that you've worried about, the load that you carried, you will now ask yourself, "How come I don't have any more burdens?" You won't be able to do that with your kind of surgery. You can only do it with the type of surgery the plants provide." So there's a lot of respect on both sides.

CHAPTER 6

Teachers:
Don Solon & Don Wilfredo

I THINK I TOLD YOU ALREADY that my first teacher was an alcoholic. His name was Don Wilfredo Tuanama. He had a beautiful voice. He was the perfect Master conducting a ceremony. He knew exactly when to sing and when to tell a story. That is something that's getting lost now in modern ceremonies. My teacher knew when a song or a story could take you out of your bad trip. He would tell stories about the plants; how the earth was formed. He would tell the stories in a mischievous kind of way, but it was effective. He would tell the stories, not to make a declaration about the way things are, but to play and move energy around.

I remember clearly a story he told about a jaguar — how the jaguar is so strong and the jaguar rules nature ... so it seems. But there are still other animals that are stronger than the jaguar. There's the little ant, a very, very small ant. The jaguar won't be able to eat it, but the ant can bite the jaguar and it will make the Jaguar dance with its bites. It will make him run. The Jaguar thinks himself invincible, but a little ant … it will bite him, it will make him jump. Beautiful, man, I like that.

So the old man had these stories he would tell us.

Then, he would tell us stories about the dolphins. He would say, "They are very intelligent animals and they have a very special quality. Their sexual organ has a very special scent." The scent of the dolphin could seduce a man or a woman. It's true.

When one of my teachers would invoke the dolphin during a ceremony the women would begin to moan. It's very sensual when you invoke the dolphin. That's the song that brings out attraction. It's very, very subtle.

It has been said that sometimes shamans would try to have sex with a dolphin during a ceremony but it is a misunderstanding. It is true that some people remove part of the sexual organ of the dolphin and utilize their pheromones to produce an effect. They use the word *pusanga*, which means to be enchanted, to unite pairs. That's where this story must be coming from. It's not that they're having sex with dolphins, they're taking their sexuality. No, no. I'm not interested in that sort of thing, but I have seen it done.

So the old man would tell these stories, of course the way he told them, just made you laugh. He really knew how to work the ceremony.

He's dead now.

May I tell you more about my apprenticeship?

When I began my apprenticeship in seeking curanderos, I worked with a 120 – 123 curanderos — indigenous, mestizo — all kinds of healers. There are some you can feel confidence in, or sure of, and some others you don't. When I met Don Solon, I felt I could trust him. He was very tranquil. He was very calm. I didn't care that he invoked the Virgin Mary, Jesus Christ, and the saints. What was important to me was that I could see his tranquillity, his patience and his compassion.

I will tell you a story of a man they brought to him. The man was mad. They brought him in with his hands tied. The family was scared. Why didn't they take him to the hospital so they could give him some medicine to calm down? Why did they go to Don Solon? What really surprised me was Don Solon, when he said, "Please, please untie him." He said, "Come here, sit by my side." And the old man began to sing. He sang and sang and what I could see in the old man was his compassion, his peacefulness, and that gentleman who could not be calmed down, he began to sing too! And immediately he fell asleep!

I think the qualities that make a good shaman are compassion, self-assurance, peacefulness, trustworthiness and humility. That's my way of seeing it. I could see that Don Solon was an old man. He was a very simple old guy, but when he would do his Ayahuasca ceremonies, you could feel this strong, strong power.

It was the power of the Ayahuasca, in combination with his own power. I would see him, because of his big ears and his hands and his feet, like an elephant, beautifully grounded. He also has a very pretty voice. That's what drew my attention to him. He was just very

simple and easy without a lot of extras. Unlike other curanderos who
would tell you stories of a thousand realms, or I don't know what.
He wouldn't do that. He was simply his transmission of helping.
That's all he did.

And what I liked about the old man, listen, he always would look at
the Virgin Mary. He would sit hour after hour, meditating ... looking
at her. Always. Always. He would always take time to be in connection with the Virgin Mary. That's why I still respect him so much.
That taught me a lot. Although I'm not an adherent to Christianity,
I'm not interested in judging. I have only respect. I have my own
way of thinking about things and I know he does as well. It's what
you feel inside that matters. And if you feel good with those pres-
ences, with those beings, that's fine. It's the qualities he has that
I like. Also, he would never say no. He was always giving. In his
house before, when he was stronger, more powerful, a lot of children
would come to him so they could be healed. He was always, blowing
tobacco for the children. That was his work. He was happy doing it.

I think I should explain a little bit about tobacco.

The tobacco we use in the Ayahuasca ritual has a very important
place because it's a protector spirit. That's why it's used with such
reverence and respect in so many traditions. When I smoke it, I
smoke it with a lot of respect, singing, requesting that I be healed,
that I be protected and that it heals and protects the others.

Of course I refer to pure tobacco, which has not been tampered with,
not handled by companies, by manufacturers. The other, the cigarette

tobacco is not pure. In Iquitos, you can witness how the women make the natural tobacco here. It's a very different process.

Sometimes when we drink Ayahuasca we can see that for some people it is not being effective. It's not working. But when you bring the tobacco in and you sing to the tobacco, the spirit of tobacco, and you bring it to the person, they take off. The tobacco triggers the journey. It's a protection. It protects and cleanses.

So you see we use the tobacco very differently, and when I told you that Don Solon would blow tobacco on the children, he was not harming them, he was protecting them.

CHAPTER 7

A Walk Through the Garden

PLEASE COME WITH ME for a walk through my garden. You will have to imagine a little bit, but I will go slowly. And later, we will have a few photographs to look at. OK, let's begin.

Good Morning! Good morning, Ayahuasquita.

This is the Ayahuasca vine. As you can see, for her to develop she is going to need a tree. If there are no trees she cannot develop. That is why she's called a creeping plant. When you take Ayahuasca, if you have noticed, you have visions of ascension. So there always has to be a tree.

Remember I told you that I sometimes I feel like a tree? My veins are like vines.... Symbolically I represent the tree.

Growing next to the Ayahuasca is the *chacruna* tree. One without the other doesn't work. It is true they don't always grow that close to each other but it is a symbolic marriage between Ayahuasca and chacruna, and a marriage between oneself and the plants.

How do we know it is good chacruna? We know by the spines on the back of the leaves. The more spines, the more potent are the effects of the chacruna.

The Ayahuasca is what produces the dizziness, and the chacruna produces the visions. The chacruna has two hundred varieties but only two will work with Ayahuasca.

How do the curanderos know if the vine is Ayahuasca? By trying it, by tasting it. Chew it. It is bitter. You will feel numbness in a moment. It is like an anesthetic.

How was it discovered? By trying it. That is one of my hypotheses. I think we spoke on the first day of my interview about how the curanderos develop the vision, the sight, to discover these plants. First, they observe. They observe the animals. For example, I have a video of a jaguar chewing Ayahuasca leaves. When the jaguar eats the leaves, it goes into a trance. Generally, the jaguar is a carnivorous animal. Why does the jaguar like this plant? It likes it because it modifies his consciousness. You can see that while the jaguar is in trance, it is as if he is laughing or smiling. He flips around and rubs himself on the earth. Thanks to the animals we get a communication about the plants. Man first observes and then he begins to experiment with the plants, but he does not know the dosage. The curanderos kept trying and kept trying until they found the right dosage and too often they died in the process. Thanks to the curanderos experimenting with dosage we have this knowledge.

One has to know. It is not anyone who can do it. I can say, Alberto, go find some Ayahuasca, and who knows what he will bring. One identifies it by the taste. You have to taste that bitterness.

If you will notice, the flower of the Ayahuasca is like a butterfly. The wind disburses it and it flies.

I want to talk a little bit about the plant medicine. We don't have to be analytical about this. Chemists can tell you what compounds are in an aspirin but the curandero's vision is nothing like that. It's holistic. First of all, where does it come from? Who prepared it? What was the intention behind it? Is there water? Is there fire? Is there gratitude toward the earth?

Curanderos are always observing. For instance, let's look at this plant in front of me. Is it a tree? Is it a vine? That tree grows from the top to the bottom. First it was a vine and now it is a tree. If you look carefully inside the tree you can see a palm. Slowly the vine strangled the palm and that's how these plants co-exist. That's the way it is. One will take the other so it can live.

One has to be very receptive in observing nature. For instance with this tree, its fruit is only eaten by certain kinds of birds. They poop on a tree and in the excrement they deposit a seed on a leaf and the vine begins to grow down. It grows down, down to the earth and that's how it begins to grow into a tree. It is all interrelated, everything. That's the observation of the curandero.

So, what does this tree do? If you break a bone it can weld the bone together. I am telling you this from experience. Also, I gave my partner this plant after she gave birth. I gave it to her to drink because when you give birth all those tissues are torn. What this plant does is repair the tissues. It regenerates the tissues of the person it heals. The name of this plant is *renaquilla*.

Now we have before us a tree in the family of the *sanangos*. It is another very good teacher plant. How do the curanderos identify this tree? They do it by the sexual part of the plant. You can observe that it looks like a phallus. It is the fruit of the flower. Some are also scented. One can verify its identity by the color of its resin, which is white. Mainly, the sanangos are identified by the seeds of the tree or the color of the resin. This tree, when you drink it, you boil the bark.

Here is another sanango. If this one has no resin, how do we take it? We don't cook it. We put the bark in alcohol and let it marinate for a week. Its name is *chiric*. Chiricsanango. Chiric means cold in Quechua. When you take it, it produces cold in your body and after thirty minutes you immerse yourself in water and the heat and cold in your body are rebalanced, but you have to be very careful. You cannot take this every day. If you drink too much it will make you ill. It's for sexual potency for men and women. This is also a very good teacher plant and will bring you visions.

Now, listen, there are two ways of taking it. One way of taking it is with alcohol and the bark. You let the bark marinate for a week and then you add some honey. This is one way of taking it. This way doesn't require a specific dieta. And you can take it as many times as you want.

The other way to do it is with the resin from the bark. You get the resin and add some water. We don't cook it. This way requires a dieta. In a week's time you take it twice only. It is very strong with the resin. And you can only take it maybe once a year — two doses spread out by one week.

Here is another plant called *ajo sacha*. Ajo means garlic and sacha means wild, wild garlic. The folk people use it when they want to hunt. Sometimes they will drink it or sometimes they will bathe in it. When they bathe in it the human scent is disbursed so they smell like the plant, then the animals will approach them.

Look at the relationship between plants and humans and animals. It is symbiotic.

Another little tree, another teacher, is the Sangre de Drago. Blood of the dragon. It is so called because its leaves resemble the tongue of a dragon and its sap is blood red. Its Latin name is *Croton lechleri*. If you touch the sap it will numb your hand. Its medicinal properties are used for internal and external ulcers. Also, if you get a cut, you disinfect it and then put a few drops across the gash and very quickly it will create a scar. Same thing happens internally. If you take too much of a dosage it's toxic to your body. Recently a friend of mine took too much Sangre de Grado. Consequently he got an obstruction in his colon and had to go to the hospital. He took too much. He took twenty drops. You must take only a couple of drops.

When there are internal ulcers, you cut a plantain plant, then you carve the trunk and get the water from the cut. This water we gather and we mix it with the drops of the Sangre de Drago. This is what we drink. I have seen people get healed from ulcers and gastritis within a month. It's very good.

There is another way to prepare this remedy and it is thanks to Dona Sarela that I learned to prepare the plants a different way. First, you cook green plaintains, and with the broth from that you mix two or three drops of Sangre de Grado. You see immediately that it begins to heal.

Dragon's blood was one of Dona Sarela's favorite plants. She would mix it up with *chuchuhuasi* and other strong plants. I was always happy to visit her because she knew what she was doing and was successful with her plant combinations.

First of all she would take your pulse. It's like when the Chinese doctors take your pulse to gauge your yin and yang energies. They gauge how you are, your blood pressure, if your blood is good. This is a beautiful diagnostic method of traditional medicine. "Oh, I see you are ill in this organ," or, "Your heart is not well" or this or that. She always took the pulse first. From there she could tell how the person's spirit was, whether a person could be healed or not. Then she would collect various plants and the bark and resins from the trees and prepare the plant combinations. She would mix it and cook it really well, and the plants would do their cleansing work. Many women who had tumors in their uterus would be told by the doctors there is nothing we can do for you. They were more or less telling them to just go home to die. So as a last resort they would go to see Dona Sarela.

In these cases the dieta is of utmost importance. All the restrictions of these dietas, restrictions of certain foods, staying away from sexuality, staying away even from the scent of other people, all these restrictions are very, very important. When you take plants you become very sensitized. All your senses are opened. All these restrictions contribute to the healing. I have seen it — I have seen women who have been told they were going to die in a month, but after taking the plants, slowly the tumors disappeared. They would go back to the hospital and the doctors would be amazed! "How did this happen? What did you do? What did you drink?" They would say, "I drank the plants with Dona Sarela." After that the doctors themselves would go to her for consultations. They wanted to work with her.

So what did we learn from that?

Thank you! Thank you to the plants. They heal us. They cleanse us. They make us aware of our own spirituality. Thanks to the earth. Thanks for all this nature. It makes us conscious and aware. This garden is here for a reason. Our creator has made it. It is a garden full of mysteries. And the illnesses are also a mystery. Thanks to the illnesses themselves we become aware of where we are not well. And that is where Ayahuasca and the plants really help.

Icaro # 2 De la Ayahuasca

*(*translation)*

Ayahuasca maman	Mother Ayahuasca
Taqui taqui muyqui	I sing to you
Chuya chuya jampipuni	Always crystal clear is your medicine
Misqui ñucño cuerpo chaita	That leaves my body sweeter

Ayahuasca rampi manta	First blossom of Ayahuasca
Taqui taqui muyqui	I sing to you
Chuya chuya jampipuni	Always crystal clear is your medicine
Misqui ñucño cuerpo chaita	That leaves my body sweeter

Ayahuasca sapi manta	Roots of Ayahuasca
Taqui taqui muyqui....	I sing to you....

Ayahuasca shungo sito manta — Heart of Ayahuasca

Ayahuasca lucerito manta — Ayahuasca of the stars

Ayahuasca cogollito manta — Flowers of Ayahuasca

Ayahuasca cielocito manta — Celestial Ayahuasca

Ayahuasca chacrunera — Ayahuasca and
Chacruna, sister spirits

Ayahuasca tikunera*

Ayahuasca of the tribes
I sing to you
Always crystal clear is your medicine
That leaves my body sweeter

CHAPTER 8

A Visit to Pablo

Pablo Amaringo has been a very good friend for a very long time. He used to be a shaman, yes, he will tell you about it, but I am going to let Michael tell you the story of our visit to his studio and our day with Pablo.

We will resume after our visit to Don Solon and to Julio.

Michael:

Our first day in Pucallpa, Don José took us to the studio of renowned visionary painter, Pablo Amaringo. They are old friends. Don José has enormous respect for Pablo, so much so, that he wanted us to meet Pablo and learn about Ayahuasca visions before even starting the interviews for this book.

For many hours Pablo took us on a rapid journey through his own visions. Like a jazz musician he was riffing, taking us here and there, dropping bombs of big ideas into our consciousness. He was very generous and true to the Ayahuasca visions — we were not going to land anywhere.

These are some of the stories he told.

Pablo:

I was twenty years old, and at that time I was painting pictures of
my mother, portraits of friends, animals, and landscapes but when
I became a shaman I began to see other things about painting. In
reality, I did not know anything. So Ayahuasca taught me.

When I worked in the Capitania I did not believe in anything. I only
believed in what I could see. "There is no God. There are no spirits.
There is nothing."

I got sick in my heart and was sent to the Capitania for treatment.
But there was no improvement. They would give me pills and vials
every day. I did not want any more remedies because I was going
crazy. So I told my mother, "I am going to look for my medicine.
If I do not find my medicine I am going to stay there and die." So
I went to this place near Tamanco and there I saw my father who
asked me what was wrong. "Take the Ayahuasca," I was told. "And
take a strong *soplando*. So after taking the Ayahuasca, ten minutes
later a healing doctor came to operate on me. He cut my bones here
and there. He turned to my chest and pulled out my heart. He moved
arteries around. He moved my heart around and said, "This vein here
is bad. I am going to heal it." So he cleaned it really well. He rubbed
something like a gum on it and that was it.

The whole thing passed and I went to sleep. The doctor said, "Do
not work tomorrow, do not force yourself, and take everything slow."
But when I awoke the following morning, I felt like I was never ill! I
felt really whole. I gave up my former work.

Well, now I believed a bit, but thought the vision must have been like a fever. It was the properties of Ayahuasca that healed me but I did not want to believe. The doctor said, "After your healing, we are going to give you a white cap to take care of you." But I never saw a white cap so I forgot about it.

Nine years after my healing my sister got sick with hepatitis. At the hospital we were told to bring her home so she could die at home. The following day she was on her deathbed. She had not eaten for three days. I told my mother, "Tonight my sister is going to die. I am going to fix our home so we can have a good wake." I got out my saw and my hammer. I went to the living room and there was a man and woman there. I asked them, "What do you want?

They said, "We know that there is a woman dying here and we came to heal her."

"No, it is impossible," I said, "I know you are healers, but she is so far gone she does not even speak."

The lady responded, "I want to see her."

I said, "No, not anymore, even my mother does not want you to see her."

So this woman said, "If your sister can tolerate my incorporation and my concentration she will get up, and if not, your sister will die."

So my mother approved. They were going to do everything possible to heal her.

The couple found her to be very young. Poor child. The woman requested that her husband sleep by her side so he could help her.

The woman asked for a tall glass and got out a fistful of chopped tobacco. She put the tobacco in the glass. She also noticed some garlic, lemon juice and onion broth on the table. So she filled the glass with this juice. She added drops of camphor and florida water, just a few drops. She got a packet of arsenic and put this in the glass as well. She mixed it with her finger. I thought she was going to give this to my sister. Instead, she braced herself and took the drink. I said to myself, "This woman is going to die right here!"

I was scared. But before she drank she put some camphor in her mouth. She said, "Let's wait 5-10 minutes and see what happens. So we sat. After 5 minutes she asked me, "Have you ever taken Ayahuasca?" I did not want her to know that I had because who knows what is going on right now, you know?

So after 10 minutes or so she looks at me and says, "You are lying to me about Ayahuasca. You have a white cap on your head!" Then I remembered what the "doctors" had told me many years ago.

"You are going to help me heal your sister," the woman said.

"But what am I going to do? I know nothing of these things," I said.

"Rub her arms."

So I did. "But madam, my sister is dying. I do not want to bother her."

"Rub her arms," the woman said. My mother came in and she began rubbing my sister's legs.

After about half an hour of singing and soplando, soplando and singing, the woman sung so prettily, my sister's eyes became focused. So the woman asks my sister, "What are you seeing, my little one?" "I see an angel above my headboard," my sister said. The woman kept singing. She told us to keep rubbing my sister. After about another half hour, we are about an hour and half into this now, the woman asks my sister, "What are you seeing now?"

"Now I see a virgin up in the firmament on an altar," said my sister.

The woman proclaimed, "She will be saved. She will be saved." The woman kept on singing and my sister returned to sleep.

"Prepare her a big meal because she will wake up very hungry," this woman said. She had not eaten in several days. And from there I began to think that there is something else going on here. How could they have awakened my sister who was on her dying breath? I could not deny it.

The couple left. The woman had to be cleansed for she had taken on my sister's illness. "I've got to go purge myself of her sickness. I will return at 9 p.m. this evening with several other shamans." These other shamans were not well and she had to work on them. There was a total of 20 people who accompanied her when she returned. So that night she gave me Ayahuasca to drink and that night I received all my powers, but I did not know how or why. The only thing I did not learn or ask the lady was how she'd prepared the Ayahuasca. Just a quarter of a litre was shared by all of us and we drank it by the spoonful. She gave me half of that amount.

I wanted to run out of the house screaming. I was going crazy. I did not know what was happening to me. Then a band of angels came to me that I could see very clearly and said, "Pablo, do not worry, we are here to protect you." I could see the angels so clearly, how they were dressed, their auras.

I saw all these rugs made of all kinds of colors that were brought to me. I was dressed like a king. They put belts on me. They put brilliant shoes on me. They put my crown on me. They were all female beings. There were also two princes.

A month later I was thinking of drinking Ayahuasca again. My mother said, "Close the windows for there is a dark storm coming." The storm passed by us instead and then I suddenly began to sing the woman's icaros, her songs, and in Quechua, which I did not speak.

What happened to me was a rare thing, but the spirits know, they know.

From then on I began to feel the ills of other people. People were startled that I could do this. I was not examining them with an apparatus, but I could feel where they were sick.

You know, I was a very good shaman. Sometimes, during the day, a hundred and twenty, a hundred and eighty people would come to me for healing. The same thing would happen at night. That is why I drank everyday.

Yes, I was a very good shaman. I could fix anything. If a robbery occurred I knew who did it. I never charged money. But people would give me money or tobacco. I never went to the bank. I put it all under my pillow.

Certainly, Western artists will benefit from taking Ayahuasca since each one of us has a gift, a way of seeing. Each person is his own world.

I always had communication with spirits. People would hear stuff moving around in my room and they would take a peep, but they would not see anything. I can see spirits like I am looking at you right now.

I was a very good shaman. I would ease the people's pain. I was very apt at healing. I went to Huanuco, Cuzco and Iquitos to heal. I went to a lot of places. But I also watched my movements because at that time being an Ayahuasca shaman was against the law and I could end up in jail.

When you work with the medicine you can become a healer, but you can also be given the powers of a *hechicero* (dark witch), but I did not want to use those powers. I wanted to use my powers for healing. So what happened? When I healed the victims of the hechiceros, they wanted to kill me. For a while there, they could not dominate me while I was in the city, but when I went to the jungle they attacked me and I went crazy. I would feel crazy for about two hours inside the jungle. I did not know who I was or where I was or who was around me. So I returned to the city to see who could heal me. Several curanderos came to see me, but they did not want to get involved for it was not five hechiceros that attacked me, but twenty-five. An elder who had taken Ayahuasca for many years, he was about 90 years old, he said to me, "Pablo, I know that you know a lot of things, but if you want to continue this work you will have to kill each one of your enemies one by one. Each time you kill one of them you will be stronger. Kill them or they will kill you at any moment." But during a dieta I felt so much pain at the thought of having to kill them that I retired instead.

I have always been a curandero, not a hechicero. I saved so many people. But once you retire you have to leave it all alone. I do not regret retiring. No, now that I am this age, it would have been very painful to know that I had killed so many people.

After that I just painted — landscapes, animals, my mother, mythological figures, representations of the shaman and so on. I did not paint my visions because that would cause me to be ostracized — people would talk about that kind of stuff.

I painted my visions when the scientists asked me to do so, Dennis McKenna, Terence McKenna and other scientists.

Initially, they just admired my art. They liked my landscapes. They were sorry they had not met me before. They had been through Pucallpa eight times. I asked them what they were doing here, "Are you tourists? Students?" In those days we did not see a lot of tourists around here and they said they were interested in the magical plants of Peru, both from the Sierra and from the jungle. So I asked them what plants they were looking for. They mentioned *toé* and Ayahuasca. "Ah," I said, "I know what you are after!"

I told them, "Many years have gone by and I do not do that anymore. I really am sorry. I cannot drink anymore or give you drink. I am clean from all of that." They were very sad and disappointed that I was no longer doing Ayahuasca, but I said I could paint all that the spirits have shown me and from there I began painting. This was in the 70's.

I have taken some pain from painting my visions, and I keep quiet about it. I do not tell the folk around here anything about this. Some people have said that I am filled with demons and so forth. I have felt bad about this.

But here is my book! *

Look at this young man! Now I am 72.

Ayahuasca will reveal to you all the matters of the spirit. Everything has a spirit, a spirit for a song, a spirit for a poem. The spirits made me see so many things. Ayahuasca is great medicine for all the creations. It is good for the artist, for the musician, for the scientist, for the sculptor, for the mystic, for the religious person. It is good for all. Ayahuasca allows you to feel what things are, the spiritual life, the physical life, the life of the waters.

I could have lived anywhere on the planet but I always prefer the jungle.

---

* *Ayahuasca Visions: The Religious Iconography of a Peruvian Shaman*
By Luis Eduardo Luna and Pablo Amaringo
North Atlantic Books, Berkeley, California

Michael continues:

The next time we visit Pablo, I present him with a white Tibetan khata. He puts it around his neck, and even though it is 90 degrees out, he never takes it off. He tells us of a vision that he had had that morning.

Pablo:

"I got up very early today, at 4 o'clock in the morning, I am very happy, because I had a vision last night of a white light and white beings descending on me … and the fact that you gave me the white khata reassures me of that. I saw people … lots of people. I was sitting on a throne, and was surrounded by all these beings. All these folks came and surrounded me with light and glory. I feel so happy and give thanks to the Diving Being.

I am so glad to have had that dream. I felt well-loved and embraced by this light and all these people. I have not wanted to go back to sleep since then, and now I find it very special that this khata is given to me."

Michael:

Pablo shows us painting after painting, each one more spectacular than the last. Quietly he says, "I have to show you one more, but I won't finish it until tomorrow". When we see it, there is a collective gasp. It is alive. A curandero riding a jaguar seems to leap right out of the canvas. It is a masterpiece and Pablo's last painting.

Pablo bequeaths it to us and allows us to buy it. He instructs us to keep it covered and only look at it once a month because it's that powerful! We can show it to certain friends but, as he says, "It is not for profane eyes". We ask, "When we die, should we give it to a museum?" He says, "No, give it to someone you love, because my spirit is here, my essence."

As our visit to Pablo comes to a close, he gives Geraldine some comforting words regarding her mother who has been in and out of hospice for about a year. He turns to her for a moment and says: "Don't be too sad about any of this. Okay? Don't be too afflicted by it. Recognize that the time to let go will come when your mother is ready to let go. Energetically, we still have our umbilical cord tied to our mother. Every son and every daughter is connected to the mother by an invisible cord. You have to be very present about what you're doing with the work. You have to hold your space to let her do what she needs to do. Do not resist what's happening. I sense some level of resistance, but let that be. Once your mother is dead, you'll have your own cord to yourself. Whatever you're doing energetically, your mother knows, she is picking it up. But, because you're umbilically tied to her still, it is very important that you hold your space. Let her do what she needs to do, do not resist what's happening.

Wow...

"I love to talk about these things because they're real but they're not material and yet we feel the influence vibrationally. That's why, when you're with somebody whose vibration is not right, you also get sick.

"You know, I felt you coming. Way before you got here ... your strong vibration ... I knew you were coming, I could feel you. I felt you were a good spirit. If we did not have the good spirit and the good vibrations that we all have, I would be doing what I usually do when I am not comfortable with someone's vibrations, which is walking around, being polite, but trying to quickly get that person outside my field."

As Geraldine and I stand up to leave he gives us both a long lingering hug. Pablo's face is in total bliss. Then he says, "For the rest of my life I will be in your hearts," then he pauses and adds, "No, even after, I will still be with you."

CHAPTER 9

Ceremony

Geraldine:

The next morning Don José picks us up in two *motocarros* piled
high in the back with all the accoutrements of the shamanic ritual,
his rattles, his flutes, his crystals…. Today, though, he is without his
chacapa. It has been stolen along with many other ritual items.

Never mind.

Michael, Alberto and I, along with José and the musician Artur Mena,
climb into the little back seats and careen through the dusty streets
of Pucallpa sending up clouds of red dust as we plunge into every
available pothole. Through the wild chase along the back streets and
jungle paths, we arrive shaken, but happy.

Don José has several places where he conducts his ceremonies.
Today we enter a large circular space with polished tiled floors and
a mandala ceiling. There are only the five of us and we quickly
pick our places around the perimeter and arrange our cushions and
buckets, just in case. Michael has his own chair, King of the Maloca.

I sit nearest the door, then Alberto, then Michael, Artur, and across from me Don José, who is setting out his ritual objects. Today he has a plastic bag filled with fresh coca leaves, which he offers us. I take one, but find it awkward to chew. I drop it into the bucket next to me. Don José has lit his *mapacho*, his jungle tobacco. He cleanses himself, then stands and blows smoke to the "four corners" asking for blessings and protection for the group.

Michael is the first to go up to the "altar." I photograph him as he lifts the small glass with his two hands to his lips. He does so with reverence and gravity. He goes back to his chair and we look across at each other, two cosmic astronauts about to lift off, Godspeed, Michael … Bon Voyage … Alberto is next, Alberto, the humming-bird, the poet, the musician. He seems to dance up to the altar to receive the sacrament. I can never see how much he drinks, he always seems so present during a ceremony, able to play the most enchanting music on his exotic instruments, delicate and subtle. He must know the secret of how to gauge his energies. I am still at my own mercy.

My turn next. Do I walk? Do I float? I don't know how I get there. At one point half way across the tiles it feels like the "last mile," like "dead man walking." I've been here before. I've experienced luxu-riant bliss and abject terror. I resolve to do the only thing possible, I surrender myself to whatever Mother Ayahuasca wants to show me. As Don José says, "What else can I do?"

We settle in, rearrange our cushions, make note of where our shoes are, where the water supply is, sit back and wait for La Madrecita to offer us her teachings.

CHAPTER 10

Visions

Alberto's Vision

At the maloca in San Lorenzo, I open my eyes and listen to the wind.

My own bleached bones are studded with gems, orchids, humming-bird feathers and the eyes of jaguars. They are used for conjuring by the Dark One who paints herself with minerals of Blue. Near the misty river there is a Black Stone. On the Stone a dragonfly is awake.

Suddenly I pass through a yellow fog, through turquoise ether and I become Apamaneuk from Mesoamerica, Costa Rica.

I, Apamaneuk, the one who changes skins, was walking through the jungle forest when I saw a secret game. An eagle, regal and sharp had landed on the lush jungle soil. From beneath the leaves and vines a salamander snake swiftly rose up and with its bite poisoned the great bird. The salamander snake vanished as quickly as it appeared.

The eagle soared up to the vast empty sky and I instinctively pursued through vines, mud, leaves and rocks, the great bird above me.

Eventually, I saw it land near the rapids of the river and I waited to see what would happen next.

There were many plants from which the eagle ate. I camouflaged myself within the shifting shades of the jungle light and intently studied the spectacle before me. Late in the afternoon the eagle hopped, skipped, flapped its wings and took flight once more. I watched in amazement how the eagle soared free of the poison through the silent blue. I ran to my village and told elders, children, men and women of the events of the day. We all went down to the river where the sky-earth-plant communion took place. We have used the plants ever since to be sane and strong, to dance and chant.

I look at Michael and Geraldine, each deep in their entheogenic cocoons. I am moved by Michael's courage. He is breathing in deep and letting go deep. Michael is inside the opulent demands of shape shifting momentums. He is trying to repattern his central nervous system through the dark thick brew. He is tinkering with delicate evolutionary strategies of our neuro-cognitive architecture. So am I.

I know that Ayahuasca will take you to places you need to go for healing and release. The plant communes with you very personally. Reports of a communion with a divine alien other are well known in the academic literature.

There has been a ruby-breasted bird singing. The blood feathered one and I are in conversation. I relax and let the understanding delicately arrive.

I am completely naked by now, except for beads around my neck and a sun tattoo on my chest.

I see Geraldine to the left of me. I look at her and see her enveloped in transparencies that are mossy and at times rain like. She herself is luminous. At this time she is smiling. Lightening strikes around the maloca, accentuating private intimacies being shared between her and the transparencies. A "storm system" is passing through — literally and inside whatever our limbic, mammalian and neocortical brains are creating atmospherically.

A few years ago, near the very end of a magnificent initiation, I saw a giant albino serpent with human ears swaying majestically in front of me. I was both in awe and startled by a power that was gazing straight through my eyes and into my soul.

Pablo had said that, for the Shipibo Indians, encountering their Serpent God was a sign of great attainment. I did not quite know how to integrate this understanding into my humble life. I had been with a rainbow serpent during this ceremony as well.

The air, the ambience, is charged with particles, invisible sparks, magical ions. Wind currents pass through the maloca. They take us in further to nonvisible truths.

As we chanted to an Indian drone instrument DJ was playing, a palatial weather system seemed to be summoned that, we agreed, passed by like the Mother star ship, like an exquisite and sublime procession of stellar and cosmic offerings that came through with the thunder and rain downloading subtle teachings for each one of us individually and across many scintillating eons.

I stepped out of the maloca at some point. The ruby-breasted bird cocked its head in a branch nearby.

Michael's Vision

The shaman shakes his rattle. He whistles, breathlessly. His seductive voice weaves through me with beautiful and eerie icaros, which create openings in my brain. I remember to focus on my intention. I am here to learn, to go deeper. I breathe slowly in and out. I feel the gritty, molasses thick medicine of Mother Ayahuasca ripple through my belly, my liver and kidneys, and then jet up my spine to my brain. She is present. It's time to ask. I think, "Show me Divine Love."

Faintly, at first, with hardly any color saturation, geometric images appear. It brightens and becomes something.

I see a yellow-peach colored gauze. I feel there is something behind it. Slowly, Mother Ayahuasca pulls back the veil to reveal a soft yellow room. I realize it is a nursery. Curiosity draws me near. I try to focus on this amazing vision.

As I look closer, I see a womb-like room, secure and comforting. How strange. Why would She show me a nursery? And like any nursery, which may display the first A-B-C letters of the alphabet or a fanciful mobile for the new arrival, this too has pre-school teachings. Everywhere, in this room, is the support and love of all the child's previous ancestors going back to pre-history.

As I move into the room, I began to see that the designers of *this* nursery have prepared the most fantastic and elaborate carvings — too vast for the eye to take in, except in short gasps, for the being who will arrive shortly. Behold the sacred! Complete and total awe! The carvings are perfect and stretch on as far as I can see. It's as if ten thousand craftsmen have been commanded by a King to carve for ten thousand years. It's as if generations of the universe's most accomplished artisans have been told a Divine Child is coming and to get the room ready. And they have done so. That's what I see.

These intricate carvings ... far more advanced than the Taj Mahal or anything in the Forbidden City... are sacred scriptures in Sanskrit, Egyptian, Hebrew, Arabic and many other texts I don't recognize. The walls are filled with knowledge that the child will absorb in its life. I am trying to take it all in and remember it because it's the most extraordinary place I've ever been. A heavenly palace.

I move closer into the room and can feel the breathing presence of two huge black boas that encircle and protect the room. I can't see them but I can feel their warm, deep electric hum. I think to myself, "Oh great, giant snakes." I was afraid I might see them and be terrified. But as I breathe again I find out I am not afraid. The Giant Snakes are here to protect the Child. "So who is the Child," I ask?

"You are the Child. This room is for you."

Overwhelmed, shocked, stunned. No words can describe the feeling! I am worthy of the love of the Great Mother Ayahuasca! She has poured her most magnificent creativity into preparing and creating this room for me!

I try to take it all in. I noticed the room has expanded on the far side. I can see an entire cityscape built with the same exquisite crafts-manship and intent. This is only one room of thousands, millions! Nothing is spared in Her generosity for the Child.

A second deeper wave of realization comes over me. All humans are Divine Children. She provides for us all. We are already living in a Paradise!

Hours later, when the vision has worn off and I look outside the maloca at the green field where I've been sitting, I see every leaf a masterpiece — like the carved detail in the room. Mother Ayahuasca has poured the same love and creativity into providing food and beauty for all human life. We live in an exquisite paradise. We should fall to our knees in appreciation for our sacred Earth and Universe.

This nursery was one of many visions. I wrote about it first because it was the most exquisite, gentle, and beautiful, but to balance things, and to try to express something of what one can be in for, I'm going to include here an earlier journey, just to give you an idea of the possibilities.

This journey was filled with an energy so great, it had the force of a great tsunami washing over me, and it went on for hours. It started with a beautiful landscape of jewels, and a woven electronic blanket

of undulating snakes with extremely garish orange and green colors.
Nothing subtle about Ayahuasca's taste in art! The detail was incredible and there was too much to watch.

When I first saw the landscape, I thought to myself how beautiful
it was to look at. Just then the relationship between my vision and
me shifted. Subject and object merged. Duality was gone. I was
the vision. I *was* the mesh of energy and jewels and snakes that I
was seeing.

That's when the scanning began. It was like the medicine plant had
a lot of entities working for it, and although I couldn't see them, my
body was being scanned and sliced and diced in every direction, as if
through a giant cheese grater. Later, I realized what I was describing
could have been interpreted as an alien abduction.

It was not frightening, but it was overwhelming. I certainly hoped
they knew what they were doing. I felt my DNA, my entire operating
system was being reprogrammed — and fast. Billions of terabytes of
information was shuttling through every cell.

I breathed through it, trying to stay centered. I found I could ask the
plant questions and get immediate answers either verbally, or visually
or telepathically. But there was so much energy that, for much of
the time, it was all I could do to surf the wave let alone try to carry
on a master-student conversation. I am not sure, but I may have lost
consciousness, as there is a vast amount I don't remember.

Sometime later I saw other images of organic green and flesh-colored
entities. I guess they were life-forms but more alien than anything we

might see at the bottom of the ocean. At first the light was beautiful, but when I looked deeper into the shadows there was real evil, and it was terrifying, and I tried not to look. Wrong. The lesson being taught was that good and evil are part of the same thing, and like it or not, they come in the world of duality as a packaged deal. I tried to accept this and breathe through the realization. Even though I didn't like what I was learning, I saw it was true.

Sometime later I entered black murky smoky hell worlds of scrapping electronic sounds and metals. A smoky substance rose like one of those black snakes that kids light on Halloween. I can't remember if I'd been purging then, but I may have been seeing my toxins being released at a cellular level.

All the time the energy poured into me and through me like a fire hose, pummelling me. So much so that I felt that my energy would be depleted and I would truly be annihilated. I tried to sit up straight in a half-lotus posture and breathe in and out. I was nauseous and vomited several times over the next four or five hours, but little came up because I had eaten very little beforehand, so what was purged was probably toxins from my organs.

Once, as I leaned into the bucket, bright colored pearls — like pop beads — came out of my mouth. The torrent of energy continued to hammer me. Occasionally there would be a one-breath break, and then, back into it. There is no resisting this force, which is the same as the force of Creativity and Destruction combined. Everything is constantly being born and dying. This force brings everything into being and recycles it in death. I was tapped directly into the main power current of the Universe. All Powerful does not describe it.

Beyond massive! And it is surging through me constantly. I am a part of it. Everything is a part of it. Our existence depends on it.

I was on a mobius strip dying and being reborn again and again and again and again and again and again …. It was painful, and frightening, and dizzying, and like some out-of-control carnival ride. As much as I begged, the operator wouldn't let me off. Nightmarish.

I was sure I wouldn't make it. I had nothing left. Still I fought to hang on to my last drop of energy, but in the face of Ayahuasca — the most powerful — *resistance is futile*.

When the ceremony ended, I stumbled back to my room heavily intoxicated, shaking, weaving, and dizzily dropped into bed. But the visions continued and I was hammered for another seven hours. I realized that it was foolish to have eaten so little before the session because I had no fuel and no reserves. I was feeling dehydrated, but was too weak and sick to reach the few inches to the bottle at the bedside. It took enormous strength to reach it and suck a few drops. I felt that if I didn't nurse myself back to life I'd be dead by dawn. I wanted to get someone to bring the shaman and have him end the journey. Even though I could hear others nearby I was too weak, too near death, to call out to them. At 7 a.m. the visions stopped. The journey had lasted 12 brutal hours. Short in Earth Time, an Eternity in Experiential Time.

Geraldine's Vision

The taste of the bitter brew still lingers, a combination of molasses, wheat grass and gasoline. I shudder against my will and take another swig from my water bottle. I close my eyes and wait for the images that I have come to expect, the building up and construction of the crystalline palace that seems to emanate from my own body. Slowly the structure begins to take on solidity. I see that the palace is studded with jewels and multicoloured glass. Butterflies cast flashes of red and blue and yellow upon my arms as I reach up to make my ascent.

At the first vaulted opening I recognize the form of a small child I had met earlier. She is twirling, dancing lightly and gracefully in the air above me, exulting in her ease of movement, her escape from the little malformed body that has her captive in this reality. I am so grateful to see that in her dreams she is beautiful and free and in love with herself. I feel my heart breaking open to her and to all children … everywhere … everyone.

I move through this opalescent liquid air to the next platform, where I stand at the edge of a balcony and look out into the thick fog. Gradually, a Royal Barge comes into view and I am carried out further to the edge of a river. There is sandy soil under my feet, between my toes, and reedy growth brushes my body. There is a tall thin man on the barge dressed in robes and pharaonic headdress, and I realize that Mother Ayahuasca knows all my interests and is giving me this great gift of participation! Ah! But not today! I say. I want to go higher still!

As I say this, five pale yellow serpents rise up before me smiling suggestively, swaying and nudging each other and smirking. They wear crowns with three points. "If you WANT to know, WE created humanity," they giggle. They sway and smirk…. "WE created YOU as our TOYS!" Then they indicate with their glances for me to look down. Spread below is a circus or carnival scene, tents and ferris wheels, merry-go-rounds and clowns. "Everything you do, all your inventions, are TOYS of the TOYS! HA, HA, HA!" They smirk and wink and slide out of view.

I hear the vigorous dry rattling of a chacapa and try to open my eyes. But there is no chacapa, it is the wind blowing every tree for miles and miles around the maloca, shaking their dry leaves for us. Rattling their leaves because Don José's chacapa was stolen. The wind flings the door open and the dry leaves come dancing in like welcome visitors. Then rain, like music, every drop distinct. I look up to the ceiling of the maloca and I find I can see right through it. We laugh and raise our arms, all of us are involved in the most intimate communion with the weather. Like a lover, the natural world makes a passionate response to our enjoyment. The more we appreciate, the more it gives.

I look further up through the maloca and see huge faces in the parting of the clouds. They look down on me and smile. There are men and women with fabulous jewelled headdresses. They have beautiful intelligent faces and they carry something like jagged spears. They are speaking to me, telling me they are the creator gods, Earth gods. And to punctuate their sentences, they fling out the jagged spears, THUNDERBOLTS! At the end of every sentence, POW! Over the cloud goes the thunderbolt, and we are all shaken in the maloca with the grandiose flashings and crashing. We cheer them on. More lightening! More thunder! We are all in this grand communion. We whistle, we sing, we raise our arms, and all the little birds sing too, and the chacapas of the wind, and the rain, and the thunder, in beautiful mutual adoration. Don José laughs, "Wow, Cool!" Artur plays his guitar and sings his wonderful songs, Alberto and Don José get out their instruments and play and whistle to the birds, and the birds whistle back. I feel I'm in heaven and close my eyes....

I am gradually aware of something cold and hard under my feet. I find myself standing on a rocky outcrop under a tremendous glass dome. I notice there is someone familiar standing just outside the dome. I look more closely and realize with a shock that it is my father, standing as he did in the photograph I have of him as he waited for my mother on their wedding day. He wears the uniform of a US Air Force pilot, just like the photo. He just stands, waiting.

Then I notice in the valley far below, my mother, in her white flowered housedress, walking very slowly toward the opening in the dome. She is bent and each step seems painful. I call to her but she is so far away she doesn't hear me. I take note that, with each step, she seems more upright, she seems to get younger as she walks toward the opening. I call to her again....

A voice behind me says, "By the time she steps into her place beside your father, like the photo, she will be young and beautiful again. It will be their wedding day. They will step into their new life as if all this hadn't happened. There won't be the tiniest gap from one moment to the next. Your father will NOT die in the war this time.

It will be as if all these years did not exist. YOU may not exist. It will be an entirely new life for them … one of an infinite number of lives.

And then the voice came closer, and said with a "wink," "THAT'S why the universe is expanding!"

I open my eyes to see Don José sitting next to me. I look long and closely into his eyes. He has the eyes of a jaguar. He looks right down into me and I feel very safe and very grounded. "How are you, Geraldina?" he says. I can't speak but I want him to know I appreciate him being there just then, so much. I nod and he gets up to check on the others. I look over at Michael and see that he is still working very hard on something. His breathing is deep and purposeful. He clutches the arms of his chair. I know he is going to be wherever he is for a long time yet. I want to go to him, but I can't stand up. I look at Alberto. He is smiling and stretching his arms.

I see the sun tattooed on his chest.

CHAPTER 11

A Visit with Don Solon

Alberto:

Don Solon is 92 years old. Last year he fell and fractured a hip. Up until then Don Solon had been conducting Ayahuasca ceremonies.

It is interesting that all these elders, including Don Pablo, live in relatively humble places. Don Solon is no different. Don José, on the other hand, has capital and assets.

The house is small and the living area where we meet has a large window with iron bars protecting it.

So we walk in, and there is the old master, sitting in a rocking chair, his legs lifted in such a way that his bare feet, up in the air, give the impression that Don Solon is aboard some space ship command post in flight.

I suppose in some ways he is. He has entered early stages of Alzheimer's apparently.

Inside shadowy sockets, his eyes scintillate and his smile is warm.

There is a picture of the Virgin Mary on a back wall. A few chairs surround him as he holds court from the middle of the room.

Don Solon is taken care of by one of his daughters and a son, both of whom obviously love the man. I did not sense any fear or sorrow about Don Solon's condition. They were loving and sweet all the way through our stay that afternoon.

I eventually approach Don Solon and sit next to him and just try to be with him. Somehow I metabolize my own aging and decline, death, even, by being with this elder, that is luminous and sweet. His skin is very thin and the skeletal contours are salient. There are blotches all over his skin.

Inexplicably, Don Solon seems to recognize me, and smiles. He starts telling me all these stories and seems happy. I listen and nod, not really sure what language he is speaking, yet I listen and understand. Perhaps we are now communing through an ancestral memory for Don Solon revealed to me the secret formula for controlling wormholes using rose petals, stars, and the indigo marble note of an iguana.

Don José then sits next to him. Geraldine discreetly photographs the meeting. Other folks come and visit Don Solon while we are there. He is happy to be surrounded by all these friends and neighbors. This community protects its elders.

Don José says that Don Solon worked a lot with the Virgin Mary as an ally and that ceremonies Don José attended would take place in a small back room, even though the TV was on and other chores were being performed in the household at the same time. The old man must have seen thousands of people commune with the Vine of the Soul over just as many ceremonies.

I ask Don José what teaching came from Don Solon and DJ replies that he learned to hold space no matter what goes on in the ceremony. He learned *confianza*, which in English translates as "confidence". Yet in English, many of the connotations of deep being, with presence, faithfulness, groundedness and steadiness are not as immediately evident and nuanced as the Spanish word retains.

To hold space means to keep the intent of the vision of what the ceremony is, regardless, but it also applies to how you go about in the world outside the ceremonial space.

On the surface that sounds simple, yet keeping a positive momentum, maintaining balance, repelling, summoning, shifting ethers, while 20 individuals, more or less, are undergoing massive existential and spiritual shifts, is not for the uninitiated, anxious, or unclear.

DJ learned a way of presencing from Don Solon. What accomplished shamans are doing in a ceremony is just holding a space so that participants recognize their own authentic potency, the famous mariri, the essential power in us all.

As we were getting ready to leave, I approached Don Solon. He touches me and smiles almost imperceptibly.

I can still see the Old Shaman surrendering from an emerald throne to galaxies and realms at mind-blowing velocities — free and at ease.

CHAPTER 12

A Visit to Julio
or a Buckaroo Bonzai Man

Geraldine:

Don José brings Julio to meet us at the Iquitos airport, and after a bit of hotel shuffling we all go out to eat at a restaurant on the Plaza de Armas. We order several jugs of *camu-camu* as we converse through Alberto, who must translate back and forth, even the jokes.

Julio is on the faculty of Pharmacy and Biochemistry at the National University of Peru, specializing in biochemistry, photochemistry and taxonomy. All his work is related to the knowledge of the plants of the Amazon.

One of the first things he tells us is how he cured his own cancer by creating a plant brew that contained renaquilla. He drank it every morning for a month until the tumor was gone. He brings out a limp, much folded piece of paper, signed by his team of doctors to verify the fact.

Julio is not only a biochemist, he's also a writer and a musician — a Buckaroo Bonzai Man, Alberto calls him.

The next day, Alberto rides with Julio on the back of his motorcycle on the way to a café where we are all meeting to talk together, and record whatever Julio has to say.

Alberto says we missed the best stories, which were shouted back to him as they roared down the dusty roads avoiding the potholes and motocarros and little kids in the streets.

I ask Alberto to tell me, but he says they are too hot for my ears.

Earlier in the day, we take a walk through the jungle behind the University. We bring a student along with us who hacks away at the undergrowth wherever we go. We stop to admire a flower and the student hacks away at the foliage to get to the flower, then he accidentally hacks off the flower. Everyone is upset. The poor student tries to stick the flower back onto the stem. It's a lovely flame-colored flower called, *The Devil's Ear*. There are lots of things around here called the Devil's this and that.

Julio tells us that according to the Cocamas, the world was made by a devil named Supay. For them, the devil is a good character ... a benevolent character. He is not one who engenders evil, and while the devil in Christian mythology smells like sulphur, in the Amazonian mythology, the devil is fragrant. There is a tree that produces a fragrant fruit that is known by the name of Supayocote.

We continue to walk through the jungle learning the healing properties of hundreds of medicinal plants, eventually we all collapse with
the heat.

We all repair to a shady patio at the back of the café, owned by a
friend who has provided us with jugs of fresh orange juice. Don José
takes possession of the hammock while the rest of us take a seat in
the shade. We ask Julio to relate some of the myths he has discovered
during his travels among the indigenous people with whom he has
spent a great deal of time.

This is the story told by the Huitotos from the lower part of the
Amazon. It is a story about the *huito*, which is used by the villagers
to paint their faces with a dark violet dye.

"A very pretty village girl fell in love with a young man whose
heritage was unknown in the community. The mother had not been
introduced to the young man as he showed up only at night after she
had retired. So the mother said, "Today you are going to introduce
me to that young man and in broad daylight!" So they went around
the village looking for him, but he was nowhere to be found.

So the mother said, "Go gather the fruit of the huito while it is still
green. Prepare it and have it ready for when he arrives. When he
comes, put your hand in the liquid and place your hand on his face
to leave a print." So the young girl did as she was told. The next
day the mother was determined to confront the young man with the
handprint on his face. Again, he was nowhere to be found. But that
night, a gigantic moon rose in the sky and on the face of the full

moon was the handprint of the maiden. "Ah," the mother cried, "It was the moon who was trying to deceive you!"

Julio has many myths referring to plants. He says that when things cannot be explained by ordinary means, they are attributed to the supernatural, in this next case, the "devil."

There is a plant that grows in the primary jungle that always maintains itself without any grass around it, and it reproduces itself in a particularly aligned and orderly way. So the folk people say, "Who cultivates this plant? We have never seen anyone maintain this part of the jungle. It is so well ordered, so well distanced." And since they do not know, they say, "It must be the "devil." So this plant is called "supay chacra."

Julio regales us all afternoon with stories of the plants and eventually we move on to discussions of Ayahuasca. Julio makes the following observations regarding the growing popularity of Ayahuasca tourism:

"I must say that there are a lot of shamans out there, but very, very few understand what it means to work with Ayahuasca. I know people from North America who are calling themselves shamans but it is simply good business for them. They often resist what Ayahuasca will put you through; they resist the vomiting, the diarrhoea, or the terrible anxiety that can take over. Whoever can resist that, they think, must be a shaman. They don't know anything about the plants or the environment or the ancient concept of healing. They cultivate no spiritual or psychological discipline, so this type of so-called shamanism is merely exploitation.

"Indigenous curanderos know the secret of the plants and are very keen observers. They must have knowledge of psychology and the ability to give confidence. He should be able to calm a person down just by putting his hands over him. A person who can do that is in the category of shaman.

"Ayahuasca is a way to give people the power of critical awareness. It strips you down in order for you to see the path you must walk. I'm very certain of that. The last time I journeyed was 2006. I think one knows intuitively when to stop. At that point other spiritual disciplines can take over.

"The tendency toward intoxication, whether it is alcohol, tobacco or Ayahuasca, is inherent in human beings. What are retrieved and repeated with Ayahuasca are ancestral experiences, so there is no reason to prohibit the use of psychotropic substances. It is the flight of the creative imagination that gives meaning to life and Ayahuasca augments that possibility. Also, Ayahuasca is a preparation for death so that we will not fear death as we do. Like the Tibetan Book of the Dead, Ayahuasca is a practice that helps you to live well and die satisfied for having accomplished this. One finds in death the beginnings of a new life. Death is a transcendental step towards immortality that will result in another kind of life. We live in order to die, and we die in order to live. This is much like the Buddhist wheel of life and death. In this sense, Buddhism is more philosophical than Christianity. I believe that there is a deep spiritual intertwining between Amazonian indigenous groups and the culture of people from India and Asia who practice Buddhism.

"There is a spiritual richness that is maintained by the influences of psychedelic or entheogenic drugs that not only calms your pain, but your supreme anguish as well."

Our visit to Julio was coming to an end. Don José had said that he and Julio had known each other for a very long time —"We constantly feed off each other. There is a relationship of teacher/ pupil that is mutual. Sometimes there's a thread we explore together. We complement each other. What matters is that there's an equality in all of us doing this work and in sharing what we learn from the work. That's one of the features of good Ayahuasca use. Excellent. Yes."

Icaro # 3 De Las Tribus

Tikuna murayai
Muraillo murayai
Danza danza adelantito Tikuna yari
Limpia limpia cuerpecito huankinsito
Tukui Tukui yariri almacita
Tukui Tukui yariri cuerpecito

Tribu Tribu curakaini
Shamuriri shamuriri
Danza adelantito Tikuna yari
Limpia limpia cuerpecitos huankinsito
Tukui Tukui yariri almacita

Huambiza curakaini
Witoto curakaini
Koto Auca curakaini
Kashibo curakaini
Bora Bora curakaini
Piro Piro curakaini
Machigenga curakaini
Campa Campa curakaini
Cocama curakaini
Aguaruna curakaini
Chayahuita huarmicita
Aguaruna huarmicita*

(*Translation)

Tribes of the jungle
Tribes who are powerful and mysterious
Dance in front of me
Cleanse my brothers' and sisters' bodies
Cleanse their soul
Cleanse their body

Chief of the Tribes
I call your spirits
Dance in front of me
Cleanse my brothers' and sisters' bodies
Cleanse their soul

Chief of the Huambiza Tribe
Chief of the Witoto Tribe
Chief of the Koto Auca Tribe
Chief of the Kashibo Tribe
Chief of the Bora Bora Tribe
Chief of the Piro Piro Tribe
Chief of the Machigenga Tribe
Chief of the Campa Campa Tribe
Chief of the Cocama Tribe
Chief of the Aguaruna Tribe
Female Chief of the Women of the Aguaruna and Chayahuita Tribes
I call your spirit
Dance in front of me
Cleanse my brothers' and sisters' bodies
Cleanse their soul

CHAPTER 13

Death

LET US CONTINUE.

The question of how taking Ayahuasca informs our understanding of death is a great question. Yes. Nice.

When the Spaniards came, these rituals of curanderismo and the usage of plants were, in their thinking, thought to be something profane. The word, Ayahuasca, has a particular meaning: "Vine of the Dead." That's in Quechua. But there was another language that is not Quechua. Yes. There was a dialect. In the dialect, Ayahuasca does not mean "Vine of the Dead." In the dialect it means "Drink of the Soul." That's what Ayahuasca means. You ask the culture of the Shipibos or the Shuars — they will define Ayahuasca as the "Drink of the Soul." But the Spaniards forced the definition because for them this was a profane ritual. "This is the work of witches. It's something satanic." In some chronicles that is the meaning of Ayahuasca. They wrote whatever they wanted, at will. So they kept the name, "The Vine of the Dead." That's one side.

There is a relationship with death, however, because when one drinks Ayahuasca ... I don't know if you have had a death experience in ceremony, but that can give us fear because Ayahuasca makes us confront death. What I see in my experience is that death follows life like night follows day. Today you are born, tomorrow you die. It's the same thing. The sun rises, in the night it disappears. Moment by moment it gives you that kind of experience — you're born, you die, you're born, you die, you're born, you die....

And such is life.

So the definition of death doesn't really exist. It's just simply a step. That's what Ayahuasca makes me understand every time I drink. Live, die, live, die. My problems die, and it makes me live. My problems die, and I live. That's my way of seeing it.

I'm going to tell you one of the experiences I've had.

Once when I drank Ayahuasca, she very gently explained to me, she told me, "Look, I give to you, but I take away." So I insisted, "What do you give me? And what do you take away?" She said, "I take away defects and I give you responsibilities. I take and I give." So think about that. Meditate on it. "I take away defects and I give you responsibilities." From there I understood that it's the same as, I live and I die, I live, I die. That's the way I see it.

Consciousness, however, never dies. It's *always* there. It's always there. That is what I see with Ayahuasca. I feel that Ayahuasca takes away the masks we have and it shows you who you are.

Another way of approaching this is to ask if during an Ayahuasca journey our consciousness enters a realm that is an after-death realm. I would say that, in part, this happens, yes. Let me elaborate on it in the following manner: What does the Ayahuasca journey really mean for me? Well, it's similar to when you sleep. It's the same thing, I must tell you. It's like a dream. What happens is that your mind has an experience and you rest. So you are relaxing, you're having a dream. Ayahuasca is similar. You drink Ayahuasca and you experience something similar, but with Ayahuasca it is amplified so much more.

The other day, I had an experience with renaquilla — I was very tired, I was very fatigued. So I went to sleep in a hammock. It was so gratifying, so nice! I rested so deeply that Ayahuasca visions began arriving! I began to experience stars, lights, in my dreams. Well, let's see, I'd rested for about an hour. I felt so full that all my problems, all my worry, my fatigue, had vanished. I felt fresh, fresh, fresh, after I woke up. I said, "Wow! This is so nice!" And I tell you, in the dream I was living, it was like an Ayahuasca trip. That same day, I had a ceremony. It was very easy for me to enter into the other world very quickly. I drank very little and very quickly I entered another realm. And there, the dream that I had, the rest that I had, made things easier, and I had an amazing cosmic journey! I felt the cosmos was in my body and then I began to sing. And many of the people thought that out of my mouth, with the songs, came shooting stars. They could see that. And I could see that! I could see that in my journey too. And I was grateful for that dream! Thank you for that rest. I relaxed, I could release. During the ceremony it was very, very easy. I couldn't feel any of the weight of other people. So for me, that ceremony was cosmic. And I could see entities of light that would enter into people. And they could feel it. "What is this?" I wondered, "This is strange, but so pleasant." And that's what I was seeing.

I will also add that encountering ancestors in the other realms during our journeys is most excellent. I've had such experiences. Let me share with you a couple of things. Six or seven years ago, I was at a ceremony in Lima with a group of friends. I was experiencing the journey with a lot of visions, and I want to tell you first what happened to somebody, and then what happened to me. During the journey this gentleman, a psychiatrist, began to feel the sickness of his father. His father had died of pulmonary cancer. I could see something dark, something black in his back, so I came near him and I sang to him and I cleansed him. I made him throw up, expulse that cancer through the vomit. And he felt something like flames coming out of his lungs. He told me later, "For years I couldn't understand that I was carrying this load from my father. Now the Ayahuasca has shown me that I cured the cancer that killed my father." So what does that tell us? Well, that the problems or the things that our fathers carry can get transmitted to us. At the same time that we're healing ourselves, we're healing them as well, the dead, our beloved. That's what I have felt. And that gentleman felt the same thing when he expulsed the cancer. He felt a liberation, a freedom in his lungs and he could see it clearly.

That's why I say, "Thank you, Ayahuasca. Thank you."

So you can see what kinds of dimensions Ayahuasca reaches. Now I'm going to talk about my experience with my mother. I was deeply into my journey and I felt that she came to my body, and I felt inside my body that she had had some kind of bronchial problem. I was thinking, "Why does my mother have to be inside me now if she's already dead?" The Ayahuasca told me, "It's because you have to solve this problem and work on it." It also said, "It's the same thing that happened to the other gentleman." And I had to catch hold of the sickness of my mother. I had physical symptoms, but with Ayahuasca, it freed me. It freed me, and it freed her. After that she gave me a smile. Ah! Wow! How good! How good!!!

From that experience I understood more how Ayahuasca is a holy plant. It is a privilege to partake of Ayahuasca. I would have loved for my mother to have taken it. Ah, too bad she died. But, as her son, I've had the opportunity to drink it. I've got the Ayahuasca spirit. This is it. You're healing yourself, but you're also healing your mother. You're healing yourself but you're also healing your sons. You're healing yourself here in the present, and you're also healing the past. Ayahuasca prepares us across times, the past, the present and the future. And to me the present is to be here now, and feeling it fully. And so I say, "Thank you, Mother, that you have granted me to be a full man, a complete man so I could experience and feel all this, and play with the worlds, experiment with the worlds."

Yes. That's just the way it is. One can have access to all sorts of realms and times. It's such a mysterious plant with a very deep mystery. Sometimes it is very painful because when you drink it and you see those things, does that not cause you pain? But later on that pain is relieved because you're also healing. You know, these things are all part of the shamanic practices.

The ritual of Ayahuasca for me is very simple. Intention is important. You could be thinking yes, I'm going to see an ancestor, yes, I'm going to see this and that. I'm going to prepare ahead of time. My intention is such and such. But suddenly you're not going to see any of that. Because what Ayahuasca does is very spontaneous. What arrives for you will always be timely. When you least think about it an image or insight will appear and then you say, "Oh yes! How this shows up!" There you are not utilizing your reason. You just allow, you're just allowing it all to happen. Yes.

I'm going to talk about another thing that happened to me since we are speaking about all these matters. Somewhere around the fifteenth time of having drunk Ayahuasca, I began to feel a very deep sadness and I began to cry. You know, I would ask myself, "Why do I have this sadness? Why am I crying?" And all of a sudden, without thinking about it, the image of my brother appeared. And then I saw my brother was dying. I said, "Is this real? Is this true or not? I don't know!" I felt I was purging myself of all that sadness and I kept crying. But I stayed with that question. The ceremony ended. Three or four days went by and what had happened was true. My brother had died, had physically died. But years had passed since I'd seen my brother. I hadn't seen him in ten years! How could I have known of his death? It wasn't the exact hour he died. But I could feel his death. I could feel he was dead. And truly that had an impact on me. From that experience I realized that Ayahuasca is able to take me to another dimension, so that I could enter other worlds. Worlds of ... let us call them ... the dead.

There are people who are very sensitive and they can have experiences of this sort without the use of Ayahuasca. Normally, what Ayahuasca does, is amplify whatever latent powers we have. And it's faster. That's what the plant does. That's what this holy plant does. Yes, it is worth noting that drinking Ayahuasca is a practice that can prepare you for your death.

I'm going to tell you a story of the experience of a person who came to me. The only thing she wanted in her life was to drink Ayahuasca. She had a cancer that had spread all over her body. So she came to work with me. I could see her. What I said to her was this: "You are coming here knowing that at any time you can die."

"I know that, but to me it's very important to drink Ayahuasca," she said, "because I feel that I'm freeing myself from this cancer. I'm liberating my spirit so I won't remain trapped within this illness." She said, "I'm conscious, I'm awake."

And I could see that she was. I said, "You have two weeks. You're going to leave your physical body. I could see a light that was flowing from her. From the diet, she came out luminous. I simply told her, "You've got two weeks left. Physically, you'll have to leave us. But now you've done some work for your spirit. Said and done."

Two weeks later she died. Physically.

Later, I found that she had left some pretty words, "Thank you. The only thing that I wanted, the last thing that I wanted, was to experience or live Ayahuasca. Thank you."

So every time I drink Ayahuasca, I'm preparing for death. That's been my impression. When I drink Ayahuasca, it's a preparation for death, and at the same time it's teaching you how to live well. How to live in a delicious way!

CHAPTER 14

Dietas

I WOULD LIKE TO SHARE WITH YOU a little bit about the practice of dietas.

Here, for the vegetalistas, a dieta is a type of retreat in an isolated space. Preferably in the jungle because it's there that you'll be in absolute contact with nature. There you can be more pre-disposed to understand, to comprehend how plants work with you. That is the concept of dietas for the vegetalistas.

It's very different from the concept of a diet in Western cultures. The Western concept is to lose weight, eat vegetables, eat vegetarian food. That's a very Western concept. But the concept of the vegetalistas is different. It is very simple. The simplicity lies in that there are certain prohibitions you impose on yourself. Restrictions on salt and sweets are examples of such prohibitions. This would include even fruit. Nothing that tastes sweet. Nothing that tastes salty.

That's the only way that we can learn from the plants. Sexual absti-nence, as well, is very important. Also, there are certain kinds of meat you can't eat. You cannot eat pork or beef or other animals that might be harmful to your body. We, therefore, eat very simply. We eat two types of fish. There's a fish called *boquichico*, it's a toothless fish. All the fish does is eat algae from the water. And there's another fish that we call sardine. Those are the only two fish you can eat because those fish eat food that's clean. The dieta has been handed down to us from a long time ago. In curanderismo, that's very important. Before I continue relating what a dieta is and why we do it, I'm going to tell you another story. It's a true story.

One time this North American man had a pain in his spine. He took pain medicine, but there came a time when the medicine no longer had any effect on him. So he went to consult a vegetalista. The vegetalista asked him, "Do you really want to drink these plants?" "Yes," he responded. So the vegetalista made the brew. "Here, take these plants, but I'm going to tell you what the rules are, how these plants function, what you must do and what you must not do." The North American man thought the vegetalista was speaking foolishly. So the North American gentleman said, "Okay, I will submit to the rules you're telling me." So he invited him to the plants. But before he invited him to partake in the plants he said, "If you break the dieta, the following things will happen to you: Your skin will become stained and you will have lesions in your nasal passages or in your lachrymal ducts." "Well," the man said, "I'll do whatever you tell me. I'll submit to your rules." But the vegetalista said, "I'm warning you. You must be clear on this." So he provided him with the plants. For ten days he drank the plant medicine. During those ten days he began to feel really well. The vegetalista said, "Very well, now you can return to your home, but I will remind you of what I told you.

It's very important to follow the rules of the dieta. "Okay," the man said, "I'll do it." But the North American gentleman was still challenging what the vegetalista was doing. He was a bit sceptical. So he returned home. He was okay for a couple of days but he could not stand forgoing beef or pork. So what happened? Immediately, he felt something foreign, something strange enter his body. He didn't know what it was. A few more days went by and he said to himself, "I'm going to have sexual relations with my woman." That was even worse! His energy, instead of going up went down. After twenty days he began to develop stains around his neck, around his face, and on his forehead. So the gentleman went back to the vegetalista and said, "Can you cure me?" The vegetalista said, "No. Not now. You did not follow what I told you to do."

Why did that happen? How do they know that a particular mixture of plants can produce that? And why do the curanderos insist so much on the importance of a dieta? For me it's very simple. I'm not just drinking the psychoactive ingredients of the plants, I'm drinking their spirit. I feel that those spirits stay within you and that's what the mariri is, as I told you earlier. That's the power that stays within you. Yes, I point to my belly. It is both your own power and the power of the plants. There are two ways of saying it, mariri or yachai. It's the same thing. It's the power, it's the force, it's the same as Chi in Asian cultures. As you can see, this story comes from my own observation and my own experience. When one has experienced it, one knows. When one has not experienced it, one cannot really talk about it. It's one thing to have it written in a book, yet the important things, all these things have not been written about. But I have a living text, by seeing that gentleman who teaches me while he's in front of me and he knows also by his own experience how he's been taught. He has transmitted the information to me.

That is the vegetalista's concept of the dieta. Let us continue.

During this period of isolation, you have space, you're alone, you seldom speak. During those days one does not wash with shampoos or traditional soaps. You can't brush your teeth with toothpaste. When we begin to do the diet, we begin to sweat and sometimes very disagreeable things come out of us, but that's part of the process. Accept the odour that comes out. We often mask it with the fragrance of some perfume. But as time goes on, you continue, and the bad odour goes away. You begin to acquire sometimes the fragrance of the plants. For the folk people who live in the jungle, it is an aid in hunting animals. It's a way of life, you know, of subsisting, to hunt or to fish. Those folks will drink plants called ajo sacha for eight or nine days. What happens is that you keep drinking the brew and the plant keeps cleansing you. As days go by, you feel that the odour of the plant is permeating your body. I'm telling you this from their experience, what they have shared with me. Once they're done with their dieta, their aim gets keener for the hunt and the animal approaches them because the human scent is not there. They smell more like a plant, so the animal approaches. There's another word that is involved with fishing. They say it turns you into a *mitayero*. It refines your energy so you become a better fisherman. I don't know why, but the results tell the story.

There is something else that happens that's very important. When one is undergoing a dieta, there are plants that awaken you sexually. One feels heat in one's basic parts. One feels strong, strong, strong heat.

Quite a few will have erotic dreams. It has happened to me several times. There you can work with your energy, your sexual energy, really well. You can heighten it or elevate it. One begins to cleanse. One feels the purification in one's body and in one's mind as well. Sometimes, during my dieta, I have experienced all my sensory organs amplified much more than normal. I can smell really keenly. I can smell from a long distance — same thing with hearing. My eyes are also sharper. My tactile sense, too, is enhanced. Of course, when you eat that food without any flavour, well, it's bland. There's the little plantain or the *boquichico*, the fish, without salt, without anything fancy on it. But you're also very glad to have it in front of you, just so you can savour something, and then late at night, you'll have these dreams of having these great banquets and feasts! You're eating and munching, and you wake up and the reality is that you're just alone with a plantain and a fish! And the rice, that's it. But that's a passing thing. And that's the best way that the plants can go deeper in you, and that's where I have seen healings, even more potent healings. I'm a witness to that. It's not a space of just being alone, it's a place of being in solitude. True, one feels that the day is long, even the nights are very long, interminable … endless. Time becomes slower. You'll feel boredom. There's a moment when you can't even read a book. You read a few pages and then, "I still have so much more to go! What do I do with the rest of my time?" And I tell them, "Take advantage of it. It's precisely during this time that you should look within, quiet down, meditate, and you'll see that it's very healthy. The same thing happened to me when I started doing dietas."

I will do a dieta once a year for myself but I want to do more in the future. I like them. Eight days, ten days....

What I often do in my dietas is to concentrate on a variety of plants. Sometimes Ayahuasca is not involved at all. I just want to know how a particular combination of plants works. Obviously, I will not have visions like I do with Ayahuasca, yet I can experience the strong energies of other plants. And sometimes I can dream that their spirits enter my body. One of my teachers, Don Guillermo Ojanama, would just come over and give me his preparation of plants. "This is going to be your water, when you're thirsty, drink this." And he would bring me plantains, and if I had good luck, I would get a little fish. And he would not say many things … he would not talk to me much. Yes, I wanted some company! Just to chat a little bit. So I could be a little bit distracted. Oh God! That day felt so long! The nights felt so long! Yeah, so … it was very, very hard. But the only thing he would come and tell me was, "Just go on, continue. The plants will speak to you." And I would say, "But how are the plants going to speak to me?" And then he would laugh, "Yes, but just wait. The plants will speak to you." As time went by, as days went by, I felt the plants were talking to me. I could feel it. And slowly, icaros would come to me. It's like I could feel the words. "Oh! That's what he was trying to tell me, my teacher. And I said, "Thank you, Maestro, thank you. Now, I understand about plants speaking to me."

And after some more time goes by, you drink Ayahuasca. And that's where you're going to see the power of the plants that you have taken, now that they're in your body, and it was true. Every time that I would sing, people could feel my songs very clearly, and powerfully.

So after having taken plants for a determined period of time, then you would do the post-diet. The post-diet is even more powerful.

That's when he would give me salt, and that's where the dieta would stop. "From now on, you have to be responsible," he would tell me. "Now that you are returning to the city, you are going to encounter other energies, other types of food and you're going to be very, very sensitive. So now that you have drunk the plants, we have the post-dieta. Look, there are basic rules of discipline. So, for a month, No Sex." I was young! Oh, my! I was a young eager man with all my hormones on alert! It was very harsh. He reiterated, no sex for a month, certain foods, pork, beef, certain kinds of fish, nothing for a couple of weeks, fifteen days, nothing. And fruits, papaya, pineapple and even certain kinds of vegetables he wanted me to abstain from. "It's very important not to eat garlic," he would say. Or onion. I don't know the reason though. But, I'll go back to the idea in a moment.

I'm going to tell you another story that's pertinent. This teaching is the same in India and in China as it is here. When I visited a Chinese doctor in California, the first thing that he suppressed was garlic. And then I saw a doctor who studies Ayurvedic medicine. He told me the same thing. "Take some vegetables, but less garlic and onions." And the curanderos say the same thing. They're not telling you to deny the beneficial effects of garlic, it has a lot of antibiotics, but garlic does not go well when you're drinking plants. To me it's very odd that the curanderos told me the same thing as the Chinese doctor, and the same thing as the Ayurvedic doctor. Then I could see that this kind of knowledge is both Eastern and Western. The same thing gets repeated. For example, Guillermo Ojanama is an indigenous person descended from Andean people. But he always made the point about not eating garlic or onion. And he was very strict about certain fruits too. Papaya was one. The trunk of papaya, for example, is very weak. So one can't mix it with certain trees that are hard. They don't get along well. So I've drawn one conclusion, it's because of the sugar, it enters your bloodstream and you kind of dilute yourself. You turn a little weaker. All the curanderos, all the *ayahuasqueros*, all the vegetalistas will tell you the same thing. And why do they tell you that? Out of experience. A scientist may have another way of describing it and naming it — he can tell you about sugar count, but in the end it's the same effect. A curandero is not interested in the how it functions chemically in your body. What they're interested in is how the spirit of the plant works in your body, that's how they approach it. The more you drink powerful plants, the more strict the diet.

I'll tell you one more story. This is the story of a woman who had some tumors in her womb. She and her husband went to see a curandera that I knew. She said, "Yes, you will get healed, but it's very important that you listen to me. If you listen to me you can prolong your life, but if you don't listen to me I will give you two months to live." The curandera warned the woman and her husband, "Listen, if you want your woman to get well, please don't have sexual relations with her because otherwise she won't get healed." And so she prepared the batch of plants. It was a mixture of plants, Chuchuhuasi, among others, and she said, "With this you are going to get well, so if you want to live, please listen to me. Abstain from sex, from certain kinds of food — pork, beef." It was clear that her case was critical.

So the woman drank the plants. After a couple of weeks, fifteen days, she looked beautiful. She felt she was eliminating the tumors. She was getting rid of her illness. She could feel it. But her husband, because he saw her turning pretty thought, "I want to have sex with her." So they did and they broke the rules. Just three days before the month had gone by, they went to see the curandera. "Listen, we broke the dieta." You know what the curandera said? "Excuse me ... but I warned you. Now the plants are not going to be able to heal you. So, I'll send you my blessings, but go home. I warned you. You didn't listen."

So what does all of this mean? A plant diet is spoken about with so much passion, because they've experienced it and they know. It's such a great gift that they give us.... Yes, sometimes we Westerners cannot understand it. So I was telling you of the concept of dieta of the vegetalistas. That is the way they see how the plants help, and how it helps you elevate yourself spiritually. They won't say it'll help you grow spiritually, that is not the language they use, they'll say you will just feel better. You'll feel healed. I, of course, I say it elevates you spiritually, for that is true too. When you're in that retreat you feel these things. You're more content with nature and with yourself. So I feel that dietas are so important at times. In the world of curanderos, in the world of shamans, they say these things because of their own experience.

So yes, the dietas not only prepare you for Ayahuasca, but for other plants. First of all, I take the plants so I can have power. Spiritual power. Physical power. And of course to lose a few pounds!!! And it happens that I do lose a few pounds. But more than anything else, I take the plants so I can gain strength and learn more about plants.

One of my favourite plants is renaquilla. I'm going to tell you story about a vision I had with renaquilla. I have never written about it, I'm glad that it's being documented.

Five years ago, I was half asleep when I began to feel that there were these tribes camouflaged with leaves, and these tribes began to dance in the air. And they began to sing. They would make some sounds like *Tuvan* throat-singers. That's how they would make the sounds. Or sometimes they would strike the trees and I could hear them. I could hear the percussion. I saw it as so real. And there was a chieftain. He had a light right in the middle of his forehead. It was blue. And with that blue light, I could see the rest of the Indians dancing and they invited me to participate with them. That group of Indians with the chacapas, they would strike my body. And I could feel it, "Aaah." Sometimes it would hurt, sometimes it was kind of pleasant. And I woke with my muscles so relaxed. I could feel my spinal cord aligned. I was so happy. It was like a dream, or, I don't know what it was. That's when I drank renaquilla, and that's why I like it. I've felt a lot of healing in my body because of it. I felt looser so I could play my instruments. It was smoother to play my instruments.

I would like to repeat that again. So I will try that again. I want to try that … I want to … because I like it.

CHAPTER 15

Ayahuasca Revolution

Please let me tell you what I have seen regarding how Ayahuasca practices have expanded. About twenty years ago, there was not much interest in plant medicine. When I began to work with this plant, it was mainly the folk people who would come to work with Ayahuasca. Usually it was around health problems, but also problems of love. That was the main role that the curandero played.

At that time the thinking was that it was for people who did not have a lot of knowledge. It was mainly for folks who were perceived as ignorant, lacking culture, just simple people. That was the perception at that time. But slowly, this kind of work has taken on more importance.

When I began my apprenticeship with Ayahuasca, I was living in Tarapoto in the department of San Martin. A French doctor came to do research on traditional plant medicine. At first his research began on natural medicines with its use of fruits and vegetables and organic diets, but slowly, after many years, we began to understand the importance and the potential of the practices of the curanderos.

I would like to say, without bragging, that we were the first to begin to explore and elevate the level of what traditional medicines meant, at least where I was. We tried to understand for several years how the curanderos could heal with these plants, and with these practices.

Then I came to visit Iquitos as well. There were some curanderos around in those days. Tourists, Americans or Europeans would come by, but not so much interested in Ayahuasca. The general interest was in the Amazon. But slowly, there was more interest. So right around 1988 we had a conference here ... about traditional medicine. Here in Iquitos. First it was in Lima, then we came to Iquitos since Ayahuasca comes from the Amazon, and from then on a lot of doctors came, from Lima, from France, from the United States, from England. Also anthropologists arrived, and that's where Jeremy Narby* started. That's where this current was born. I don't know whether to give myself the luxury or the humility to say that we were the pioneers of this, I mean, the pioneers of this development.

So, right around these years, 1989, I began my travels to talk about my work with La Madrecita. There was some interest; it was innovative, and truly I think we were the first pioneers to get into this work. Now, many years later, I can see that interest has grown incredibly. People from Europe, Asia, the Middle East and China are interested in learning these practices. In some places the practice is a little more discreet, but the expansion is very, very large.

---

* Jeremy Narby is an anthropologist and author of *The Cosmic Serpent: DNA and the Origins of Knowledge, Shamans Through Time: 500 Years on the Path to Knowledge, Intelligence in Nature: An Inquiry into Knowledge*, and is the co-author of *The Psychotropic Mind: The World according to Ayahuasca, Iboga and Shamanism*. Since 1989 he has been the director of Amazonian Projects for the NGO Nouvelle Planète.

There were some problems with Ayahuasca practices in Brazil, and that's why these Santo Daime practices came up. In one way, they really opened up a lot of possibilities. And as they began opening up … they began to have difficulties … until they took the issue to court. But in the end, Ayahuasca has prevailed. Now these churches have been recognized.

There are some people who would like to stop this expansion, but they will not be able to do it. The seeds have been planted. In these last few years the people who have taken an interest in the work are doctors, psychologists, anthropologists, bankers and others. Ayahuasca has reached the elite of the planet and its reach is very wide. It first started among the humblest of people.

This is what I see. I see that the Madrecita has been travelling through the darkest places to make new concepts bloom, and to make new people head toward the light. I see it like the spreading roots of a tree.

I have a couple of banker friends, one in Spain, the other in the United States. One was vice president of the bank. The other one headed a department within a bank. When they came here to drink this holy plant, it changed the way they approached their work, and the way they approached other people. The world of business requires people to be hard and cold. What happened is that Ayahuasca began to soften them, and it made it easier for them to interact with their clients, which somehow made everything more productive. There was an interaction that was more "human to human." So they said to themselves, "What a sweet way to reach people." They were not as cold and calculating. According to what they told me, in the world of business there are certain patterns, but for them, those patterns became more pliable.

These two people used to consume other drugs so they could keep the apparatus of production functioning well. They used other substances. Of course, they were productive, but they felt they were killing themselves in the process. When they tried this holy plant, they were transformed. They left behind many defects. One of them stopped using drugs, and they quit drinking alcohol and smoking cigarettes. It became a little difficult for them to be in their regular social functions. They were now living in a different world and slowly they realized the importance of Ayahuasca in their lives. Now, they have quit their banking businesses and are dedicating their lives to the advancement this spiritual search. One practices Buddhism and mixes his practices with Ayahuasca. The other one is exploring other alternatives and he wants to learn more about this kind of work. He has noticed that he feels happy and feels happiest when he is helping others.

So, in our conversations I have remarked how great this plant is but there is also a danger because Ayahuasca moves its presence into a political realm.

I had the good fortune of knowing one of the Prime Ministers of Peru, and he was one of the President's personal physicians. Thanks to him, a law was created that made traditional medicine in Peru legal. Thanks to him. And there was a big debate — a political debate. The medical establishment was against it. The doctors were against having this legalized. They said this type of practice is very

on Jose with the Ayahuasca vine

The more spines on the leaf, the more potent the chacruna.

Renaquilla: good for repairing injured tissue.

Ajo Sacha or Wild garlic: used by indigenous people when hunting to hide the human scent.

Michael, Pablo and Alberto in Pablo's studio.

"...ablito"

"...ainbow serpents are protector spirits."

"This painting is of an Ayahuasca session beneath the earth where the elders live. In the realm above the ground is where the centaurs dwell."

"he double of the shaman is the jaguar because the jaguar is pure and sees with eyes of innocence."

The cooking pot

Don José begins the ceremony.

"Each curandero prepares the ceremony in whichever way he wants. There are no fixed patterns because one's inspiration sets the ceremony."

The painting of the Virgin Mary in Don Solon's house in Iquitos.

"Vhen he would do his Ayahuasca ceremonies, you could feel this strong, strong power."

n Solon

The Rio Aguaytia

Iquitos river scene on the Rio Amazonas

On the banks of the Rio Amazonas

Don José points out exotic birds in the treetops.

ulio Arce Hidalgo, in the garden of the National University of Peru with the plant, Granadilla which has many medicinal uses.

The little entrepeneurs

Don José with his charangito

dangerous. But thanks to this Prime Minister, this is the only country in the world where the traditional medicine is legal.

But now it's changing. Now, there are scientists who are interested in Ayahuasca and curanderismo work. For instance, Charles Grob.** I'm sure you know of him. He's done a lot of work in psychiatry around this. He's had the good fortune of doing these practices with some patients in the hospital, but sometimes it can be difficult. On the political side of things, they don't like this at all.

You know, it's usually the religious folks who are against us and that happens here too. Religion has always been opposed to these practices. They sometimes imagine it as, you know, satanic practices.

Personally, Ayahuasca expands who I am. She expands me to a consciousness of creativity. Sometimes, it is impossible to put this solely into words. What I feel is that I just simply live this.

I am going to tell you an experience I had. Six years ago I had taken Ayahuasca mixed with toé. I was invited to visit the house of this gentleman who now lives in Mongolia — Glenn Mullin.*** Glenn's house is replete with Buddhist art and deities. Immediately, I

** Director of the Division of Child and Adolescent Psychiatry at Harbor-UCLA Medical Center, and Professor of Psychiatry and Pediatrics at the UCLA School of Medicine. He conducted the first U.S. government-approved psychobiological research study of MDMA, and was the principal investigator of an international research project in the Brazilian Amazon. He has recently concluded an investigation of the effects of psilocybin on anxiety and depression in the treatment of the terminally ill.
*** A Tibetologist, Buddhist writer, translator of classical Tibetan literature and teacher of Tantric Buddhist meditation. He is the author of over 20 books on Tibetan Buddhism, most of which focus on the lives of the early Dalai Lamas. Glenn lived in the Indian Himalayas between 1972 and 1984, where he studied philosophy, literature, meditation, yoga, and the enlightenment culture under thirty-five of the greatest living masters of the four schools of Tibetan Buddhism.

said to myself, I have seen this in my own work. I felt something very powerful enter me. It was so curious. Mr. Glenn asked me, "Why are you looking at this so intently?" I replied, "In my visions I have seen similar things." He told me that the Tibetan monks, in order to have these kinds of visions, used meditation certainly, but they used plants as well, and that is never written about. To me, possibly, one of the plants taken was toé, which is *datura*. I tell you, I could feel the same kinds of experience in my own work. I realized how much plants have expanded my awareness. So there is a meeting of cultures that takes place.

Well, after this I thought maybe I am not that crazy! Ha, Ha, Ha! There are other crazy people here as well. So we can meet and speak in this language and in those dimensions. That is what I like about this work. Possibly, there are other worlds in our consciousness beyond this.

CHAPTER 16

A Plant That Unties Knots

As far as whether or not there are dangers for people using Ayahuasca and creating their own groups without a shaman or experienced guide, yes, there are dangers. But it's impossible to stop these practices.

In an Ayahuasca ceremony, the shaman is important because what the shaman does, what the curandero does, before inviting the sacrament, is he opens up a space. He or she opens up a space so people can feel at ease and confident. That's the first thing the curandero takes care of. The second thing the curandero manages is the setting where the work takes place. And the third thing ... the curandero has to have the best intention to really help people out. That's why it's important, in these plant rituals, that you have someone of knowledge and experience.

Sometimes during a journey people will get scared. So what to do? It is very simple. Sometimes these things can seem funny, but they're efficacious. Breathe ... breathe ... and let go, release. Breathe and let go. Release whatever it is that has you trapped or contracted.

Remember, let go, release. Breathe and let go, release. Don't fight it. I know that it can be scary. Once we begin to release we are liberating ourselves … liberating ourselves from fears, from pain, from sadness, from rage and anger. Release all that has us entangled.

What I like about Ayahuasca is that it's a plant that unties knots. It loosens up one knot, then another knot. It continues to untie knots and untie knots and continues to free you. And those knots are about hatred and pain and sadness, and what a good thing — to release all that, to untie all of that. Breathing well is very important. It just helps you to relax and release.

So, does having a degree in psychology, philosophy or theology benefit one working with Ayahuasca? For some people, yes, but if you go ask a person who's simple … who has not studied, all he wants is to be healed. And isn't that what everybody's looking for? Some healing? Whoever you are — psychologist, psychiatrist, philosopher — we're all in one way or another seeking some kind of liberation or healing. And the same applies to the curanderos — they're also doing that.

Let us talk about the prevalence of sexual imagery, dismemberment and rebirth in some of this work. Let's begin with sexuality. The plants always go to the first chakra. It moves that energy, the kundalini energy, which is incredibly powerful. You can feel the surge going up your spine, and then it blossoms like a lotus flower. That's your sexual power. I would like to add that the word "dismemberment" is inappropriate because what's really going on is that you're being operated upon … you are being restructured. Your way of seeing, or seeing yourself, changes. You are freed. You are born anew.

Remember Pablo's story of the "little doctors" and his white cap?

Regarding the word "devil," or "demon," or entities that want to harm us, the word "devil" has never existed within the language of the Amazonian people. Here they're called "supay." The Spanish translated it as "devil." It's neither a good spirit nor a bad spirit. The problem is, the religious people have "satanized" those entities. But they are not bad or good, you see? For example, in some songs, I invoke "supay." It's not that I'm invoking a bad entity. It's just a spirit. It's not a good or evil spirit. But there is another way of speaking about this. And this experience I have gone through.

At first I was very reluctant to believe that spirits existed. Over here we use a language that is very simple but easy to understand. We say you have taken a "bad air." So you ask yourself, what does that mean? I'm telling you this because this happened to me. I was here in the jungle, and I felt as if an entity entered my body. I began to feel dizzy. I felt very bad, like a whirlwind. I began to throw up. And then the folk people told me, "You've had a bad air." "But where is it? What is it?" They said, "It's in the ether. It goes through you, and if it attacks you, it makes you sick." To me it was just like a journey. But it was horrible because I was throwing up, I had cold sweats, my blood pressure lowered, I was hot. So I asked the people I worked with, "Could you please give me something, a pill or something?" "No, we're not going to give you a pill because that's not going to help you, it's going to make it even worse. We'll bring you some tobacco." And then they blew the smoke of the tobacco on my crown and my chest and belly, and it was like wiping it away with your hand. After that I believed that these things existed. I said to myself, "All this is very interesting." Then I went to bed and fell asleep.

In my dream I began to see who had sent me that bad spirit, you know. "Oh," I said, "Oh! I know who!" And I saw it very clearly. Before this happened to me I would not believe in any of it. This is all foolishness! But when it happens to you, you realise that it does exist.

So are there bad experiences ultimately? This is how I see it. In these practices, apparently, one can be going through a bad experience … but in reality you can't say that it's bad or evil. It's good that you go through it because you realize where the problem is within you. So I say, just submit … just submit.

I will say something else about Ayahuasca. Once you take it, it will always be a part of your life. It will always be with you. It stays in your consciousness and you are always in communication with her. Once you open that door, it is always open.

What I observe is that the Ayahuasca experience is like a key to a coffer, a chest or a trunk. And in that chest or trunk, you will not know what you're going to encounter, but at least it gives you the opportunity to open it. If you open it, you're going to find a world that contains everything. And that's what happens to everyone, in every ceremony… "Here… Here…" We have the key and we open up…. We open that chest, that trunk, that coffer. And once you open it, it will always be a part of you. Like I was saying, "Thank you, Ayahuasca." It's a privilege. It's a privilege … because it gives us the key to open up.

My friends, there is so much value in gratitude.

I say thank you for having a mother who brought me into this world. I say, "Thank you, Mother," "Thank you, Father…" because Father helped me to be here too and of course I am without judgement, without judging them. I am in gratitude for just being whole … complete … with all my faculties. And thank you for this body because without this body I could not experience what I do experience. So, thank you, thank you, thanks to it all, thanks to everything — from being an infant to being in old age. And thanks to Our Creator, Our Mother Earth and to all the elements. Gratitude is so enormous.

CHAPTER 17

Toé Is Datura

I AM GOING TO TELL YOU about a couple of experiences I had. There was this gentleman who was approximately sixty years old, and after many years of therapy, he continued to feel estranged from his own life, in a sense, alienated from his own body. So he came to drink Ayahuasca. I prepared a special brew that included some toé leaves. Toé is datura. So what happened was, this gentleman entered into a strange and frightening experience. He thought that he was in labor giving birth. He was screaming and screaming. So I told my assistants to take care of him, with time he'll slowly calm down. And the next day, when people shared their experiences, he was a bit embarrassed when he told his story. He said he thought he was giving birth because he was experiencing labor pains. So a few days went by and all of a sudden his journey came back to him, the same images and sensations, but not as intense as he had experienced in the ceremony. He became very, very scared. "Am I going crazy? Am I going to be this way the rest of my life?" So he came to me and I cleansed him and he settled down. So my friend very smartly said to him, "Why don't you ask your mother how she brought you into the world?" The older man said, "I think it was a normal birth."

So he asked his mother and she told him, "You know what? Go ask the hospital." So he called the hospital and began to ask questions. "Can you tell me where my records are, the records of my birth?"

"Yes, okay," a lady said, "I have it." So this is what he found out.

His mother had so much pain during childbirth that they gave her an injection to calm it down. It was a medication that contained the active ingredient "escopolamina," which is made from datura. Because they had given it to his mother to calm her pain, the gentleman entered the world with practically no pain at all. But all that pain his mother had felt, he took it in and brought it with him. That was why he was uncomfortable with his life. And years of psychologists and psychiatry could not address this. So what I believe really happened here is, that during the ceremony, when I gave him the toé, which is also made from datura, it triggered the memory of what had happened at his birth and so his release began. He released all that. He was healed from all of that. He said to me, "Thank you, thank you, finally I was able to let go." "Yes," I said, "But remember, it's thanks to the plants, keep that in mind."

The medicine, escopolamina, used to be administered with morphine as a painkiller during childbirth, but later it was found to be implicated in the high rate of infant mortality, and so it was discontinued.

But what is interesting here is how the toé made him relive the experience of his birth and of his mother giving birth to him. He said to me, "Thank you, I feel free from this."

He thanked his mother.

So what happens with these plants is that you can relive all of that kind of thing.

Recently, I invited some plants into two people. Again, one of the plants was toé. The toé is a very strong teacher plant. So I invited two people to drink the plants, and one of them had the effects and the other person did not. I did not drink the plants, but after about ten minutes into the ceremony I acquired all the effects of that other person. I took his journey. It was, in a way, a kind of protection of him. And in the journey, I was taken to other worlds where it was explained to me the importance of the four elements in healing.

Within the dream, the vision, I was a pilot of an aircraft with all my gear, well protected ... and in the dream I travelled to the world of water. There I began to see other beings. They were just like you see in the paintings of Pablo Amaringo or the paintings in the Mandalas of Bali book. Very clearly, I saw it. There they began to speak to me. By the way, it's very important that you approach these beings with a lot of respect, to call them with a lot of respect so that they will inform us, these teachers. So there they made me understand the significance of the elements.

To begin with, water.

All that is water, like oceans, rivers, seas, all of it is also within you; it's there within you .... Observe well, that in the rivers, in the lakes, in the oceans ... there are also living beings there, the fish, the stingrays, the eels, the sharks, the dolphins, and so on. Very well. So they tell me, "Look! In order for you to have the same vibration, the same awareness as them, you have to put it into your consciousness

that these living beings can be taken as your allies. So invoke them.
If you want them to protect you, you must vibrate in the same vibration as them." For example, the stingray, it's a dangerous animal, the
eel as well, so is the shark. They're very dangerous, no? But in these
journey states they are not dangerous. They are there for a reason.
So I was feeling that I was calling these animals with the songs
and they were coming. And they were protecting me. Whatever bad
energy was around, they were in charge of protecting me. That's the
shamanic, no? Those are the water elements and their animals....

Now, let's go to the elements of the earth.

What are those living beings that live on the earth? Let's go first
with the animals; the animals we have, for example, the jaguar. The
otorongo, or the jaguar, represents the power and the serpents represent knowledge. And there are other animals that are very dangerous,
like spiders, snakes, and even the ortorongo, even the jaguar. It's also
dangerous, no?

All those animals are dangerous. So what I was learning was that, if I
vibrate at their level, we become the same. But to continue with the
animals of the earth — ants, spiders for example —if I vibrated at
their level alongside them, if we get along well, it's because they're
part of us and we're part of them. That is so with the animals of the
earth.

There are also the plants. All plants are medicinal in reality and
some are highly poisonous, very dangerous. But again, they all can
be your allies. They're not really dangerous. Ah! What great rich
knowledge....

Let's go to the elements of fire. What do we have? Sun. The volcanoes. Fire has a lot to do with sexuality. It's the heat that we have inside our bodies. It is the sacred fire that also is our ally.

Now we have the elements of air. What are they? The wind. The hurricanes. Tornadoes. Those are the elements of air. So, when I was seeing this element of air, I saw that it was the same as the element of water because when we breathe … our respiration is water … our sweat is water. The heat that we have from the earth is what we have in our bodies. The water is in our veins, the earth is in our bones and the air is what we breathe. Those elements are within us. Sometimes we're too distant or too far away from all of this knowledge. We don't pay attention to it. If we had that consciousness we could find our healing, which is what we are trying to do. We can vibrate on those levels, thanks to the plants.

So, let's thank the plants because they teach us about that.

Remember the day when we were singing in the maloca? Yeah, the animals were hearing us. Thanks to the Ayahuasca we can synchronize ourselves to the same vibration as them, and we could sing like them and they would respond. Remember?

Thanks to Ayahuasca.

God! Thanks to Ayahuasca and thanks to this entire creation. That's why I say it's a mystery, and that's why I say we are also a mystery. It makes us discover our own mystery.

Ayahuasquita is unique. Sometimes, I laugh at how mysterious she is and how she shows you your own mystery.

The experience of Ayahuaca is very complex to explain at times. In those states what is simple is that you live it. You just live it.

I'm going to share something that happened to me. You've noticed that when we take Ayahuasca there's neither time nor space. So she made me live through a moment, maybe a minute, where my world was completely white. It was completely in white, brilliant! Oh! It was the best! It was delicious. And I understood that it could have been millions of years that I was living in that white space, yet it only took a minute. That's because there is no time.

I have seen changes within myself, that's why I take my plants, because I have become a better human being and I am of service to myself and to others. That's how it has helped me. It has turned me into a better person. That's why I take it.

For me the learning doesn't end. It always goes on. The doctorate that it gives us is just life and the experience of being alive. The other day I was thinking about myself. Now, here I am fifty years old, but I'm whole, I've got all my faculties, and I have fifty years of experience being here on this earth. What gratitude! Yes, thank you, thank you. I have all my faculties and if I go on a few more years, well, thank you, thank you! That's how I was observing myself and I thought, "As more years go by, you becomes wiser because you've accumulated all this experience that you're now living, it turns you into a wiser person, it turns you wiser".

So thank you, thank you for the plants and for my practices. Like I said before, sometimes I feel like a tree, and the birds begin to sing within me. The birds begin to sing those icaros. They are always whispering songs. The same happens with a painter. And if you are a musician, you know we are in agreement with this.

I'm going to share with you a question I asked my teacher. The question I asked him was: "So, Maestro," I said. "Who is it that heals? Who is it that heals? Is it you or who?"

So he says to me, "I'm the one who cures."

"Thank you, Teacher," I replied. "Excuse me, I'm very young. But can I make a comment? This is how I see things. Really, what the curandero does with the patient, what I do, because we all have the capacity to make things happen, is to give people the tools so they have the power to get out of their problem. I'm only the bridge. I am transmitting the power by bringing people the complete confidence that they can get out of their problem. So the teacher says, "Ha! Thank you. I thought I was the one who was healing." "No," I said. "What one does is transfer. That's all one is doing."

Each individual has his own power. As the years have gone by and I have continued drinking Ayahuasca, many people say to me, "Help me fix my problems." To me that is very interesting. "I can't help you fix your problems," I would tell them. "What I can do is to help you by giving you the tools so you can do it." This is how I see things.

Thank you.

CHAPTER 18

The Simple Thing

You know what makes me happy in this work? First of all, it makes me a better human being and I get to understand all kinds of things that happen in life. There are some days we feel kind of down and other days that we feel better than ever. I like understanding who I am. I still want to be a better person, a better human being. I want to be of service to my family and I would say, the human family. That's what gives me satisfaction. We know we're just like passing birds through here. All we leave behind are our good actions.

You know what? Sometimes I laugh and I say, "I will always stay with my simplicity. Nobody's gonna change that." And I'm not going to allow myself to get seduced by money. I could've done it. I feel it's easy to take advantage of these things. But that's not my way. That's not my way at all. I'm very clear about that. As far as being famous, I'm famous! But simply... simply so.... That's all. I'm not the great Maharishi. I'm not a guru. Simplicity. That's where the real power lies. That's the simple thing.

I want to be remembered — "How was José?" "He was a jovial guy!"
Always giving something of my life, that's all. I don't know ...
having good friends, always learning, always learning. Like I say, I've
got to keep myself always in that centre of simplicity. The rest, I'm
not interested in. Oh, sure, it's easy for me to become a Guru. But
no, forget that, forget that. All the things fall apart with that.

Let me tell you a little bit about my garden. The reason that I am
doing this is to develop the preservation of Ayahuasca.

Because Ayahuasca has expanded so widely around the world a
very disturbing phenomenon is occurring. Ten years ago, one could
find Ayahuasca growing nearby, now we have to go further into the
jungle to find it. People are not replanting Ayahuasca. The plant is
not being preserved. There is such a demand now.

In order to harvest Ayahuasca, it takes six years from planting to
maturity. It takes time. Once you cut the plant, you have to wait
another six years.

So I am making a proposal for the preservation of Ayahuasca and
chacruna, amongst others.

In order to preserve Ayahuasca or other plants, a constant supply of
water is very important. If there is not a constant supply of water,
those plants suffer. I want to take advantage of solar power so that I

can bring water to irrigate the soil. I also need a few people to take care of the grounds.

I would like to send a message to the folk people, schools, and universities. There is an irony here. At the schools they are not teaching students about the value of plants, so a lot of the knowledge is being lost. I want to contribute to the preservation of this knowledge. That is one of my missions. I want to pass on this knowledge of plants and their value. I am motivated to preserve this knowledge. But if we do not grow the plant, we can run out. It has brought benefits to many, but we are depriving the earth of this sacred plant. I too, sometimes feel like I am contributing to this depravation.

My plan is to grow the plant. Ayahuasca must be grown with care and love. It does affect the process positively.

I have experimented with all sorts of psychedelic plants. I am staying with her. She is my point of reference. In Africa, for example, I took Ibogaine. Here in Peru I have taken San Pedro, in Mexico, I have tried peyote. However, I will stay with Ayahuasca for she is a mystery to me and is much more complex.

You know, people become ill for all kinds of reasons. I think, more than anything, it is the lack of balance in our lives. One can see that humanity is sick and damaged if you look around.

Let me tell you a story of something that happened during a ceremony here last year.

I could see the panorama of what was coming. I could feel it. What we are in for here is going to be like a psychiatric ward. I could feel the insanity of the people. Sure enough they were throwing up, their expressions, ooof! It all had the feel of an asylum. So I kept singing, enduring what was being released, what else is there to do? The next morning, I began to talk about what had happened the previous night. I asked them, "How was your visit to psychiatric ward?" They all burst out laughing. The great thing about this way, this therapy, I told them, and I include myself in this healing as well, the great thing is that Ayahuasca lifts those burdens you brought with you. You came in tense and hard and now you are smiling from ear to ear. Even if the effects only last a week or so, much of that depends on you, anyway. From there I could see and feel how damaged we all are and how each person is a world unto himself. But thanks to the plant, at least during those days we spent together, people were more at ease.

CHAPTER 19

Surrounded by
Shipibo Women

Geraldine

On our last day in Iquitos, we travel down the wide, wide river in search of the elusive pink dolphin, past houses on stilts and half sunken boats, past confiscated timber and fanciful birds and little boys on the banks…. After about two hours, we come to a stop on a low sandy beach. Sitting on the wooden seats of our boat, we feast on plantains and baked fish wrapped in leaves. We sing icaros to invite the dolphins, but today they remain elusive, their pink dorsal fins barely breaking the surface of the water.

Little canoes with small children glide silently toward us from all directions. Treasures made of seeds and hemp and feathers and straw are gently handed into the boat. We all buy several lovely little brace-lets, and afterwards they row their little boats home with gifts of fish and plantains to share with their families. The eldest entrepreneur is perhaps eight.

We are all happy and relaxed by the time we get back to our hotel, just off the Plaza de Armas. And as expected, about a dozen or more Shipibo women are waiting on the steps with their beautiful textiles, which they carry all over Iquitos. Alberto and I are quickly surrounded, but as neither of us has any money, Michael sets off to find an ATM machine and all the women say to each other, "Michael is coming. Michael is coming." Like a magical chant they pass it around the circle. Those are the only English words they speak. The crowd closes around us holding out their textiles, quietly waiting for Michael to come. There was no obvious competition among them as they unfold one cloth after another. Within a few minutes we spend all the money Michael has given us, and we turn to say good-bye to our new friends. I remember, especially, one tiny old woman who stood very close to me and had the only piece of clothing for sale. It is a brown dress with pink, blue, red and green embroidery in the shape of a large blossom in the area of the heart. I decide I can't live without it.

As we walk up the steps of the hotel we see Michael standing at a desk. He's on the phone, which seems strange. Alberto and I are so excited with our Shipibo textiles, showing them off to each other. Michael turns and says something to me, which I find difficult to hear. "Within forty-eight hours," he says, "Hospice nurse … Mother resting quietly…"

I can't quite grasp it, but know I must keep very calm as we climb the stairs to our little room. I lie down on the bed. I can't breathe. I feel as if I've fallen out of a tree with the wind knocked out of me. I can't make a sound. I relive scene after scene of my earliest life with my mother. One after another, so quickly they pass before my eyes that I become dizzy. She is helping me with my nightdress, she is reading to me on the swing, she carries me uncomfortably in the crook of her arm up the hill, she combs my hair, she hangs the pink piñata on the olive tree. I see myself spinning around and around and around as she tries to take my photograph, she's calling to me, telling me to stop, still, I can't breathe. Suddenly I remember what Pablo said about holding my space. What does it mean? I sit up, the scenes begin to fade and I am able to breathe once more....

"Mi mama esta..." I try to tell Don José as he enters the room, but I don't have the words. Moments later he begins to sing his icaros. He sprays Aqua Florida on my crown, my solar plexus, my back and my hands ... and the great blow to my chest begins to subside. I hear Michael answer the phone and say, "Yes, thank you, we know..."

He knew that I had been experiencing my mother's death. I only knew I couldn't breathe....

Slowly I become aware that Alberto is in the room as well, sitting at the end of the bed. We were all sitting on the bed, present and participating in this great transition. Michael, Alberto and Don José have helped me to hold my space as Pablo had told me I must do.

CHAPTER 20

Gratitude

I FEEL A LOT IS HAPPENING IN MY LIFE WITH THIS WORK, and I am taking it on with sincere responsibility. The act of writing this book just happened spontaneously. Remember, Alberto, you called me about this proposal and I said, yes. This is all very curious to me. Thank you so much for supporting me in this work.

We will continue to have many adventures together.

Michael and Geraldina, before we met, I had a dream. I think I told Alberto about it. I had never had this kind of experience. At the beginning of the dream I began to double myself. I could see the physical body of a friend who was enveloped by light, surrounded by light. It was very, very luminous. But suddenly I realised that the friend was me. It was me seeing myself. And I was saying, "Oh! This is what I want. Yeah, this is what I want. I want to be filled with light!"

Then I could feel that, according to your own work on this earth, what one has done throughout one's life, if one has worked with honesty with all things that one has done, one can get to those states of being. And I felt so happy! I wanted to stay there! I felt very light! I felt, "I don't want to come back anymore to the earth … I want to stay here in the light!" And so I woke up very happy, happy, happy, and that was the afternoon we met. Our connection was very fluid.

Later, slowly, I began to decipher this dream. In the mists, what was given to me was this … According to what you're working on spiritually, healing, healing wounds, one merits to be in that state, one deserves it. But one has to work!

May I add a little more to this conversation about working with plants? The practice of working with plants here in the Amazon is that of going forward into spirituality. We're going to call it spirituality. Spirituality for me is what you live day by day, day by day in every aspect of your life. For me the only thing is to live fully. Sometimes you're up, sometimes you're down, that is all part of it. There is no definition. It is just being at peace.

I don't know.

Alberto, How would you define it?

"Feeling fulfilled, day by day, moment by moment. That's how I feel."

Michael?

"Bringing the sacred in."

What about you, Geraldina?

"It is a yearning for a place, a kind of union or merging."

Remember something too, amigos, Buddha and Jesus were just like us. It's the same thing. They have gone through the human condition as well. The other day we talked about Jesus. Sometimes we carry so much pain, from everything, from the family, from friends, from society. I felt Jesus curing that pain, my own pain as well. So there we are. But I don't have the need to go to a Church. I can simply see it.

Sometimes people judge you, so, you have to just kind of put up with that and let it go. I feel like I'm carrying a burden too, like Jesus did. What can I do? Always remember, like I was telling you, we're human beings. We make our errors. We make our mistakes, no one's perfect. And so we will go on. Now, I have a long road ahead of me. Besides being a vegetalista, I'm also a father. Now I'm learning a lot from my son. Yes, I learn from him. And if this is a spiritual thing, then great! How good, because I feel happy!

Very nice. It's like that.

Sometimes I don't have the words for all of this. I have gratitude to you, gratitude for everything. Every time I wake up I say, "Thank you for another day, that I'm with all my senses. Thank you, thank you." And that's it. And here we are as a family. That thanks to the guidance of these holy plants we here have found each other.

Thank you. Thank you.

Yes, beautiful people. Oh, God, yeah! Beautiful folks … but what sweet energy! My God! It was so light, and easy, and buoyant.

It was interesting. Alberto, remember, you wrote to me? I said,
"Come here!" Remember I told you guys to come here? And the
very first day we had our experience. That's where we became really
refined and in sync. Everything has gone very smoothly, without any
problems. It has been easy. Ah! I was so worried that first day when
Alberto told me he had been deported! And I said, "Oh, my God!
What am I going to do with them?" I was really, really worried.
But later on you wrote me an email. And you said, "I got the visa!
Buy me a ticket! Tuesday, I'm there!" "Ah!" I said. I was so happy to
see you!

I couldn't just put any translator there, they wouldn't have understood what we're doing here, nor the language we were doing it in.

Oh God! And thank you for sharing the transition of your mother
with us, Geraldina. Wow, what a great way. Thank you for that
transmission. I know that for now, you're going to be more at ease,
more peaceful because you did it consciously, and with gratitude. You
practice Buddhism ... just compassion ... compassion with ourselves
and compassion with others. Yes, to feel that is the best thing. That's
all I can see and feel. Thank you, Michael, for your patience and for
making this new baby ... together.

I'm going to tell you something that happened with a friend of mine.
He thought, you know, a shaman was going to come with feathers,
and with a wardrobe. He had this whole idea. And then I come with
simple pants, simple shirt. And I began the ceremony. I began my
work. It changed his life. And he said, "Look, I thought you were

going to come here with headgear, feathers and bones, but I see you're just kind of simple. I said, 'Yeah, that's my way of being.

As Don Solon says:

"The wardrobe doesn't make the monk."

Glossary

Ajo sacha: Mansoa alliacea. Wild garlic used to treat cold conditions, such as arthritis and rheumatism. Bark scrapings are mixed with water and drunk. Alternatively, ajo sacha is added to a bath or limpia to treat fatigue, aches and pains, or flu. Ajo sacha can be a source of icaros.

Aqua de Florida: Florida Water. Scented cologne used by curanderos throughout Peru as a holy water. Used in soplas, healings.

Ayahuasca: A Quechua word that translates as Vine of the Dead, or Vine of the Soul. This term refers not only to the psychoactive beverage, but also to one of the main ingredients, the Malpighaecaeous liana, Banisteriopsis caapi. B. caapi is combined with chacruna, Psychotria viridis, which contains DMT. Ayahuasca is also known, among various indigenous groups who use it in their rituals, as caapi, natema, pinde, or yagé. This plant, can reach lengths of more than a hundred meters, and a single mature vine can weigh more than a ton. The inner bark is rich in alkaloids of the beta-carboline type. The most important beta-carboline occuring in Banisteriopsis caapi is harmine, one of the alkaloids that function as monoamine oxidase inhibitors (MAOIs), which facilitates the ingestion of DMT and other tryptamines. Harmala alkaloids, from Banisteriopsis caapi, have been used to treat Parkinson's Disease.

Ayahuascero, ayahuascera: An Amazonian plant shaman who works with Ayahuasca.

Boquichico: Prochilodus nigricans. A tropical South American freshwater fish. It is found in the Amazon and Tocantins River basins. It depends mostly on microalgae for its food.

Brujo and bruja: A curandero or curandera who uses his or her abilities to cast spells for spite, envy or money. A black magician, sorcerer, witch.

Camu-camu: Most common in western Amazonia, this species produces a red fruit that is made into a tasty juice and a delicious ice-cream in Iquitos. According to Dr. G. T. Prance, former director of the Royal Botanical Garden at Kew in London, and one of the leading experts on Amazonian botany, the fruit contains thirty times more vitamin C than citrus.

Capitania: Situated in Paucartambo, Cuzco Peru

Chacapa: A medicine rattle made from dried leaves, used by shamans during Ayahuasca ceremonies.

Chacruna: Psychotria viridis. The standard leaves utilized with the B caapi vine to make Ayahuasca. Male leaves only are used; they are distinguishable because they have tiny protrusions near their tip on the underside of the leaf. Chacruna is the source of DMT in the Ayahuasca brew.

Charanguito: Tiny little stringed instrument resembling a guitar.

Chuchuhuasi: Maytenus ebenifolia, used to increase male potency.

Coca: Erythroxylum coca. Native to western South America. The coca leaf is one of the world's most effective medicinal plants, particularly valuable for the treatment of stomach-ache and altitude sickness. It gives strength, stamina, and endurance and is considered a sacred plant to indigenous peoples throughout South America.

Cocamas: Indigenous group located mainly in the upper Amazon region outside Iquitos, Peru, they number between ten and fifteen thousand living on the banks of large rivers.

Curandero, curandera: A traditional healer who utilizes the plants, Ayahuasca, San Pedro or Toé. He or she may also use smoke, stones or several other things. All traditional healers are considered curanderos or curanderas.

Curandismo: The art and practices of the curanderos.

Dieta: The practice of following certain prescriptions and prohibitions for a defined period of time in order to open oneself spiritually to the plants. The dieta involves taking and avoiding certain food. Sexual intercourse is also restricted during and for a determined length of time following the dieta.

Entheogen: A term coined by R. Gordon, as an alternative to the term "psychedelic." The word refers to the presence of indwelling divinity experienced under the influence of Ayahuasca or other psychoactive substances.

Hechicero: Sorcerer.

Huanuco: Situated in the north-central part of the country on the eastern slopes of the Andes

Huito: Genipa americana, from which a dye is produced that is used in face and body painting.

Huitotos: Indigenous group living near the Putumayo, Napo, Nanay, and Yaguasyacu rivers, with a population estimated at 6,867. The Huitotos were severely impacted by rubber production and the population was greatly reduced.

Icaro: The name of the songs sung or whistled by curanderos during their ceremonies. Many curanderos in northwest Amazonia say that they learned their songs directly from Ayahuasca, or other plants during ceremonies, and believe them to be gifts from the spirits of the plants. The icaros bring about cures for the patient by transferring the shaman's energy with the intention to heal.

Khata: Traditional Tibetan scarf offering made of cotton, silk or other materials, with auspicious symbols or mantras woven into the fabric. In the Tibetan culture, giving a khata to someone has its own significance and protocol and is governed by tradition. To present a khata, you first fold it in half length-wise, then offer it with the open edges facing the person, which represents one's open pure heart with no negative thoughts or motives in the offering.

Maloca: Traditionally, the maloca is an ancestral longhouse used by the indigenous peoples of the Amazon, each community having a maloca with its own unique characteristics.

Mapacho: The name for the various black Nicotiana species of tobacco grown in the Amazon — most often Nicotiana rustica —as well as the cigarettes made from it. The tobacco is used both as a medicinal and a spiritual aid.

Mareacion: To be dizzy, lightheaded, or nauseous. In colloquial use in Peru's Amazon, it signifies drunkenness, particularly drunk from Ayahuasca.

Mariri: Generally refers to the "power of the plants" that is ingested. Can also refer to the shamanic "phlegm" that contains the power of the plants and the power of the shaman combined.

Mestizo: A Spanish term indicating a person of mixed blood, specifically someone with both European and Amerindian bloodlines.

Motocarro: Motorcycle with a compartment behind the driver which seats three, and a shade roof covering the passengers. A popular mode of transportation in Peru.

Otorongo: Panthera onca. Tawny jaguar.

Pheromones: Chemical compounds exuded by an organism for the purpose of carrying messages between organisms of the same species.

Pucallpa: Quechua word meaning "red earth." Pucallpa is a city in Eastern Peru located on the banks of the Ucayali River and is the capital of the Ucayali region. Settled in the 1840's by Franciscan missionaries, Pucallpa was isolated from the rest of the country by the Amazon Rainforest, and the Andes, until a road was built which connected it to Lima.

Pusanga: The "love medicine of the Amazon." A special perfume with the power to attract good fortune and human admirers for the purpose of making them fall helplessly in love with the person wearing the perfume.

Quechua: It is the most widely spoken language of the indigenous peoples of the Americas, with a total of six to eight million speakers. Some speakers of Quechua call it the "runa simi," literally, "people speech."

Renaquilla: Clusia rosea, used for treating fractures or lesions.

Sacha: An indigenous word that signifies "of the jungle" or jungle like.

San Pedro: Echinopsis pachanoi, a fast growing columnar cactus native to the Andes. It grows between 2000-3000 meters in altitude. San Pedro contains a number of alkaloids, including mescaline, and is used in traditional medicine to treat nervous conditions, joint problems, drug addictions, cardiac disease and high blood pressure.

Sanango: The most well-known of the sanangos is Chiricsanango: Brunfelsia grandiflora, used in fevers and inflammation. Other sanangos include motelosanango in the genus Tabernaemontana also known as lobosanango, uchusanango or yacusanango which are used for arthritis, rheumatism and erectile dysfunction. In addition to these, there are in the genus Bonafousia and in the genus Faramea other sanangos that are used variously to treat both hot and cold conditions.

Sangre de Drago: Croton lechleri, Euphorbiaceae, otherwise known as Sangre de grado, is used to treat wounds. It has antibacterial properties and is effective in reducing inflammation. Applied topically or taken internally, it is reputed to be effective for diarrhea, inflammation, insect bites, viral infections and wounds. It is also effective in killing cancer cells and preventing tumor growth.

Santo Daime: The first Christian church to use Ayahuasca as its sacrament was founded by Irineu Serra, a seven-foot-tall illiterate African-Brazilian rubber tapper, the descendant of slaves. When he first drank Ayahuasca, a woman appeared to him calling herself the Queen of the Forest whom Irineu identified as the Virgin Mary. She told him that Ayahuasca was the sacred blood of Christ giving light, love, and strength to all who would use it. Ayahuasca was thereafter to be called daime, as in "give me love," give me light," "give me strength."

Shaman: A curandero whose work includes contact with the spirit world.

Shamanism: A range of traditional beliefs and practices concerned with communication with the spirit world. A practitioner of shamanism is known as a shaman. The word originated among the Tungus people of Siberia, but now includes any system in which spirit world communication is vital.

Shipibo: The Shipibo-Conibo are an indigenous people of Peru living primarily along the Ucayali River. The Shipibo are noted for their rich cosmology, which is illustrated on their textiles and pottery. The Shipibo community consists of approximately 35,000 people living in over a hundred villages, primarily to the north and to the south of Pucallpa. Despite over 300 years of contact with Europeans and Peruvians, and the conversion of many Shipibo by the missionaries, the Shipibo community maintains a strong identity and retains many of their prehistoric shamanic traditions and beliefs.

Shuars: In the Shuar language, Shuar means "people." The Shuar-speaking people live in the rainforest between the upper mountains of the Andes and the savannas of the Amazonian lowlands. In the 19th century, the Shuar became famous for their practice of shrinking the heads of their enemies for the purpose of obtaining the souls which were contained in the heads.

Soplo, soplando: The act of blowing a fine line of smoke or a mist from a curandero's perfumes or medicines. The soplando is done with the intention of cleaning or clearing negative energy from a person or space.

Tamanco: Situated in Requena, Loreto Peru.

Tarapoto: Is situated in the San Martin Province and is the largest city of that region. It is linked by road to the Upper Amazon and the city of Yurimaguas. Founded in 1782 by Baltazar Martinez Jiménez de Compagnon, the city is located 350 meters above the sea and has a population of 63,484 people. Tourism is the main activity.

Toé: Also known as datura. A drink made from any number of plants from the Solanaceae (nightshade) family, specifically those from both the Brugmansia and Brunfelsia genera. Very powerful and very toxic, the leaves are frequently added to the Ayahuasca preparation to increase both the potency and duration of the psychotropic effect. Principal active biochemicals are the primary tropane alkaloids: hyoscyamine; atropine; and scopolamine. The leaves, seeds and flowers, of Toé, are most often used. They can be rolled up into cigarettes or the seeds can be mixed with wine or beer, and teas can be made with leaves and flowers. It can be used to relieve asthma when smoked, used as an antispasmodic to control Parkinson's Disease, and steamed to relieve bronchitis.

Tuvan throat singers: Also known as overtone chanting or harmonic singing, practiced by the Tuva people of Southern Siberia.

The Legalities

In the United States, under Chapter 13 of the Controlled Substance Act, DMT or any substance containing DMT is considered a Schedule 1 drug, which the Drug Enforcement Administration considers to have a high potential for abuse and no accepted medical use. Anyone possessing DMT for the purpose of manufacturing, distributing or dispensing it "shall be sentenced to a term of imprisonment of not more than 20 years."

While it is legal in the United States to possess the vine of Ayahuasca, it is illegal to possess the chacruna plant, which contains the DMT. The Ayahuasca vine and the chacruna plant are combined to make the Ayahuasca brew.

On the other hand, the Government of Peru has declared the traditional knowledge and use of Ayahuasca to be a natural cultural patrimony. In the declaration of recognition, the Peruvian Government says that Ayahuasca is known all over the world as an indigenous plant that transmits spiritual knowledge and that the effects produced by its consumption are equivalent to the entrance to the secrets of the spiritual world. According to the National Institute of Culture, the Ayahuasca ritual is establishing itself as the center of traditional medicine and is one of the pillars of its identity, indispensible to the Peruvian Amazonian people. The Government states that the effects of Ayahuasca, having been extensively investigated, are different from those produced by hallucinogens, due to the ancestral use in traditional ritual settings.

The Three Halves of Ino Moxo

Written by César Calvo, it is the story of Calvo's search for Ino Moxo, the reclusive shaman who started his life as Manuel Códova-Rios, a Spanish Peruvian, who as a boy was kidnapped by a band of Amawaka Indians. As described in F. Bruce Lambs classic, "Wizard of the Upper Amazon, Córdova-Rios mastered the Indians traditional way of life that included the ritual use of Ayahuasca. In recognition of his mastery, the Amawakas named him, Ino Moxo, the Black Panther. His ability to heal with his botanical cures became legendary, and toward the end of his life, he secluded himself deep in the jungle.

César Calvo was born in 1940 in Iquitos, capital of the Peruvian Amazon. The story of his adventure into the world of sorcery and magical realism gives a powerful insight into the nature of reality.

About the Author

photo by Geraldine Overton

Don José Campos lives in Pucallpa, Peru. He has studied with over
120 master curanderos throughout South America including Don Solon
of Iquitos. He travels internationally conducting ceremonies. A CD of
his icaros (ceremonial songs) is in distribution. This is his first book.

Don José's CD:
El Canto del Tiempo
Don Evangelino Murayay
Ayahuasca Ikaros
Above Love Records

Recommended Reading

Batuan, Dewa Nyoman, The Mandalas of Bali. Los Angeles: Michael Wiese Productions, 2009.

Beyer, Stephan V., Singing to the Plants: A Guide to Mestizo Shamanism in the Upper Amazon. Albuquerque: University of New Mexico Press, 2009.

Calvo, C., The Three Halves of Ino Moxo: Teachings of the Wizard of the Upper Amazon. Rochester: Inner Traditions International, 1995.

Cruden, Loren, Medicine Grove: A Shamanic Herbal. Rochester: Destiny Books, 1997.

De Alverga, Alex Polari, Forest of Visions: Ahahuasca, Amazonian Spirituality and the Santo Daime Traditions. Rochester: Park Street Press, 1999.

Eliade, Mircea, Shamanism: Archaic Techniques of Ecstacy. Princeton: Princeton University Press, 1964.

Gorman, Peter, Ayahuasca in My Blood: 25 Years of Medicine Dreaming. Gorman Bench Press, 2010.

Grof, Stanislav Grof, M.D. and Zina Bennett, The Holotropic Mind: Three Levels of Human Consciousness and How They Shape Our Lives. New York: Harper One, 1993.

Halifax, Joan, The Fruitful Darkness: A Journey Through Buddhist Practice and Tribal Wisdom. New York: Grove Press, 1993.

Harner, Michael, The Way of the Shaman: A Guide to Power and Healing. New York: Bantam Books, 1980.

Huxley, Aldous, The Perennial Philosophy. New York: Harper Perennial, 1945.

Lamb, F. Bruce, Wizard of the Upper Amazon: The Story of Manuel Cordova-Rios. Berkeley: North Atlantic Books, 1986.

Luna, Luis Eduardo and Pablo Amaringo, Ayahuasca Visions: The Religious Iconography of a Peruvian Shaman. Berkeley: North Atlantic Books, 1999.

McKenna, Terence, Food of the Gods: The Search for the Original Tree of Knowledge. New York: Bantam Books, 1992.

Metzner, Ralph, ed, Ayahuasca: Human Consciousness and the Spirits of Nature. New York: Thunder Mouth's Press, 1999.

Mullin, Glenn H. and Thomas L. Kelly, The Tibetan Book of the Dead (Illustrated Edition). Roli Press, 2010.

Narby, Jeremy, The Cosmic Serpent: DNA and the Origins of Knowledge. New York: Jeremy P. Tarcher/Penguin, 1998.

Narby, Jeremy and Francis Huxley, Shamans Through Time: 500 Years on the Path to Knowledge. London: Thames & Hudson, 2001.

Ratsch, Christian, The Encyclopedia of Psychoactive Plants: Enthnopharmacology and Its Applications. Rochester: Park Street Press, 1998.

Razam, Rak, Aya: A Shamanic Odyssey. Icaro Publishing, 2009.

Schultes, Richard Evans and Albert Hofmann, Plants of the Gods: Their Sacred, Healing and Hallucinogenic Powers. Rochester: Healing Arts Press, 1992.

Shanon, Benny, The Antipodes of the Mind: Charting the Phenomenlogy of the Ayahuasca Experience. Oxford: Oxford University Press: 2002.

Smith, C. Michael, Jung and Shamanism in Dialogue: Retrieving the Soul/Retrieving the Sacred. New York: Paulist Press, 2007.

Smith, Houston, Cleansing the Doors of Perception: The Religious Significance of Entheogenic Plants and Chemicals. New York: Jeremy P. Tarcher/Penguin, 2000.

Strassman, M.D., Rick, DMT Spirit Molecule: A Doctor's Revolutionary Research Into the Biology of Near-Death and Mystical Experiences. Rochester: Park Street Press, 2001.

Strassman, M.D. Rick; Slawek Wojtowicz; Luis Educardo Luna; and Ede Frescka, Inner Paths to Outer Space: Journeys to Alien Worlds Through Psychedelics and Other Spiritual Technologies. Rochester: Park Street Press, 2008.

Vitebsky, Piers, The Shaman: Voyages of the Soul. Trance, Ecstasy and Healing from Siberia to the Amazon. London: Duncan Baird Publishers, 2008.

DIVINE
ARTS

DIVINE ARTS sprang to life fully formed as an intention to bring spiritual practice into daily living. Human beings are far more than the one-dimensional creatures perceived by most of humanity and held static in consensus reality. There is a deep and vast body of knowledge – both ancient and emerging – that informs and gives us the understanding, through direct experience, that we are magnificent creatures occupying many dimensions with untold powers and connectedness to all that is. Divine Arts books and films explore these realms, powers and teachings through inspiring, informative and empowering works by pioneers, artists and great teachers from all the wisdom traditions.

We invite your participation and look forward to learning how we may better serve you.

Onward and upward,

Michael Wiese
Publisher/Filmmaker

DivineArtsMedia.com

THE SHAMAN & AYAHUASCA

JOURNEYS TO SACRED REALMS

A FILM BY MICHAEL WIESE

WINNER
BEST DOCUMENTARY FILM
ALBUQUERQUE
FILM FESTIVAL

As interest in ayahuasca grows, so does the question of how to explain this mysterious phenomenon to the uninitiated seeker.

"Filmmaker Michael Wiese's latest documentary, *The Shaman and Ayahuasca: Journeys to Sacred Realms*, meets this challenge with remarkable grace. Wiese and his companions — his wife, hotographer Geraldine Overton, and their charismatic translator, Alberto Roman — go on a trip to the Amazon to meet internationally known shaman Don Jose Campos. Shot in various locations around Peru, the film explores the role of this powerful lant medicine in Amazonian culture through a series of vignettes and intimate interviews with Don Jose and several of his close associates. Each person brings a unique perspective to the emerging picture, weaving threads of indigenous wisdom, contemporary science, and existential philosophy into the complex tapestry of the ayahuasca experience. In mind-bending portraits of jaguar-skinned shamans enshrouded by seeing-eye vines, the spiritual alchemy between man and nature that takes place in the ayahuasca realms is magically revealed — a deeply introspective story of healing and discovery."

— Stephen Thomas, *RealitySandwich.com*

"This is a gem of a movie — contemplatively paced, beautifully photographed, and filled with insights into the practice of ayahuasca shamanism in the Upper Amazon. The interviews with shaman José Campos, visionary artist Pablo Amaringo — the last before his death — and phytochemist Julio Arce Hidalgo provide a solid grounding for the story of the filmmaker's own quest for healing and understanding. Poignant and moving, the film is enriched with an evocative soundtrack by Peruvian recording artist Artur Mena Salas."

— Steve Beyer, author, *Singing to the Plants*

DVD ALL REGIONS $24.95 · ORDER NUMBER: SHAMAN
ISBN 10: 0941188191 · ISBN 13: 9781932907834 · 72 MINUTES

1.800.833.5738 · 25% DISCOUNT AVAILABLE ONLINE AT WWW.DIVINEARTSMEDIA.COM